THE PAUL MICHAEL WEIGHT-LOSS PLAN

How You Can Lose Weight So Fast Your

Friends Will Think You've Given Up

Eating Altogether!

by Paul Michael

1 2 3 4 5 80 79 78 77 76

Library of Congress Catalog Card Number 75-37431

ISBN 0-688-03051-3

A PREFACE -- AND A PROMISE

Congratulations!

You have taken the first giant stride on the road to losing your unwanted and ugly pounds at last -- the first stride on the road to a healthier, longer, happier and more satisfying life. Here is your personal copy of my Confidential Report -- THE PAUL MICHAEL WEIGHT-LOSS PLAN.

Right at the start, let me make you one guaranteed promise-- this is the LAST weight-loss plan you will ever want or need!

For, there is no other weight-loss plan that I have ever discovered -- and I have spent a great deal of money and more than half a lifetime searching -- that works nearly as well, surely or as permanently as this one.

However, it is important for you NOT to judge the value of this Confidential Report by the number of pages or the number of words. After all, we've all spent money on so-called "miracle" books with hundreds of pages in them. The only trouble was that the books didn't help at all. In this Confidential Report there has been no effort to add useless material just to make it appear more valuable.

What you bought and paid for was a weight-loss plan that works -- not mere paper and ink. I'm sure you will agree that a weight-loss plan that really works is worth its weight in gold -- a great deal more than the small price you paid.

Now, I must ask a favor of you. Will you please keep me posted on your weight losses every step of the way? Let me know when you have taken off the first five pounds -- then, when you have taken off all the weight you want to take off -- and finally, when you have kept the weight off for a minimum of six months. I promise that I'll keep your name and address in the strictest confidence -- but I will be able to point to your success in my future selling efforts. You can write to me, Paul Michael, at 2525 East 21st St., Tulsa, Oklahoma, 74114.

Yes, I have a vested interest in your success. That's why I'm now going to offer you something you've never been offered with any weight-loss plan -- a FREE CONSULTATION SERVICE. If, after you have finished reading this Confidential Report you have a question about my plan, send me your question in writing along with a stamped, self-addressed envelope. As long as it is not a medical question, I'll answer it for you without cost or obligation of any kind.

But, you must remember one important thing: the TRUE value of this weight-loss plan will depend on the use you make of it. If you don't read it -- if you put it away in a drawer -- if you hide it among your magazines -- if you forget that you bought it -- it cannot possibly work for you!

Use the PAUL MICHAEL WEIGHT-LOSS PLAN as your step-by-step guide to becoming SLIM once and for all!

TO BEGIN WITH: ...

My name is Paul Michael, and although we have never met, the fact that you bought my weight-loss plan tells me some important things about you:

1) You have a real desire to lose weight or you would not have spent your hard-earned money for my plan.

2) You have more than likely tried a number of ways to lose weight before -- pills, exercises, miracle plans -- even perhaps, meditation. Some have managed to help you take off a few pounds -- but always, before you turned around -- all the weight was back on -- or you were even heavier than you were before you started.

3) You have come to the conclusion that the only thing that will really work for you is outright starvation -- forever.

Let me assure you before you read another word -- this is not the case. If you follow my weight-loss plan you do not starve -- not today, tomorrow or ever.

What's more -- when you follow my instructions to a tee:

You will never have to go on a diet again ...

You will lose weight significantly in the first

11 days and you won't feel hungry, nervous or edgy...

You will feel better every day...

When you look in the mirror you will see the years peeled away...

You will never again have the bad side effects that come from taking dangerous pills and drugs...

You will begin eating in a new way -- a way that will give you pleasure and satisfaction without adding pounds and inches...

You will become a more vital, alive human being...

You will become more attractive as well as a more effective person -- able to deal with the trials and tribulations of daily life...

You will add extra years to your life -- because you must remember -- the fat die young.

First, I'm going to ask you to forget everything you now know (or think you know) about dieting. Most diets are based on two principles. First, that you starve, and second, that your body cells starve. One does not have to be a great medical authority to see past that thinking. Chances are if you starve you are going to be upset and irritable. This is the very time people eat most. If you starve your body cells you won't be able to stay on a diet very long -- it will be unhealthy for you.

In this plan you'll eat lots and lose weight through what appears to be a change in your body chemistry. I've highlighted the important points by calling them "Paul Michael Diet Tips." These appear in capital letters and they will help you concentrate on the important points.

Let's get a few ground rules down. With this diet you are not going to be hungry. In fact you'll eat lots of good healthy food. What you will avoid is food that has been poisoning your system since you were a child. The very food that made you fat in the first place. I'm going to change many of your thoughts on the concepts of food and dieting. This report is based on a number of specific principles. They will be explained and amplified but it is important we agree on the basics:

1) You'll eat all you want ... but of different foods than you are currently eating. Your body chemistry will smarten up.

2) You will eat six meals a day instead of three.

3) You will learn the psychological factors that were involved in establishing your mistaken eating pattern and how to change them.

PAUL MICHAEL WEIGHT-LOSS TIP #1 <u>CUT OUT MOST CARBOHYDRATES FROM YOUR DIET</u>. <u>EAT ALL THE PROTEIN FOODS YOU WANT</u>.

<u>"Smarten Up" Your Body Chemistry</u>

For fifty years or more, doctors have been telling us that the body is like a furnace. It burns whatever you put in -- makes no difference if it's bread or meat or candy -- all that counts is calories. Today, with the increased sophistication of chemistry and biochemistry, I can honestly tell you <u>it's just not true!</u> All calories are not alike. I can say this even though there are still a lot of medical men around who stick to the same old line. But doctors learn their chemistry from the research men and modern research is showing us that body chemistry is a lot more interesting and complicated than your trusty old furnace.

One of the things scientists know now is that nothing turns to fat quicker than carbohydrates. Even <u>fat</u> in your diet doesn't make fat on your waistline as fast as carbohydrates do. The body, in other words, is a lot more discriminating about its "fuel" than we thought it was. Chemically, your system knows whether it's being fed starch or fat or protein, and it acts accordingly. Starch, to the body, is a storage food, a luxury food. Carbohydrates are the things that get put away for that hypothetical rainy day when there's nothing to eat. And how does the body store food? In the form of fat, that's how.

Carbohydrates are an extra treat for your system. They're the bonus you give yourself over and above what you need to live on. But if you're overweight, you don't want or need any extras. My diet plan says don't cut out any necessary foods. Don't go hungry, or starve yourself, or suffer. Just eliminate the frills, the elements your body can do without very nicely, thanks. Is it really true that carbohydrates aren't necessary in the diet at all? A lot of biochemists think so. But my diet program doesn't aim to put you on the far-out fringes of basic research. I don't want to make you a guinea pig (or any kind of pig at all!). Don't cut <u>out</u> starches, just cut way down. Maybe all scientists don't agree that you can live a healthy life with <u>zero</u> carbohydrates, but you'll have a hard time finding one with a good argument for eating <u>lots</u> of carbohydrates.

Why do I say that my diet program can "smarten up" your body chemistry? Because I'm almost sure, if you're chronically overweight, that you're living, and eating, with a lot of bad habits you've learned over the years. You've trained your metabolism to get its energy from the wrong sources, namely, starch. Ask yourself right now, "What do I consider the most basic food?" If you have a long-time weight problem, I'll be willing to bet your answer is, "bread", or maybe "rice" or even "baked beans." Something starchy and heavy. In order to lose weight permanently, you and your body have to be re-educated.

First of all, bread isn't the basic food for human beings. Meat is. "Naturally" thin people know this intuitively. The body can use proteins and fats directly as sources of energy. Some peoples, the Eskimos are an outstanding example, have lived on nothing but meat and fat for generations. Our prehistorical ancestors probably had a diet very similar to that of the Eskimos, supplemented by a few nuts and berries. Of course, people can survive on pure carbohydrates, too. The difference is that the body is "smart" about meats and fats, but "stupid" about carbohydrates.

The body, you see, will store up all the carbohydrates you give it -- just keep salting them away until you weigh 300 pounds. Even then, if you give your system starches, it will hoard them. But with proteins and fats, it's something else again. The body knows how to use what it needs of these foods and flush away the rest. Your body has a much higher protein I.Q., you might say, than it does for starches. That's why you can eat all you want on my diet. All you want of pure proteins and fats, that is. Because your body knows how to handle these foods and it knows when enough is enough.

If you're a life-long fatty, you've educated your metabolism along a certain path. Your body is used to taking in carbohydrates, converting them to fat, and storing them. New food that comes in (especially carbohydrates) is burned for energy. And the stored fat stays stored. Any extra carbohydrate today? The body thriftily stores that too, as fat. But what happens when you drastically reduce your carbohydrate intake? The body is forced to locate a new source of energy. And what could it do but start burning up those stored deposits of fat? Presto! You're losing weight.

"Wait a minute, Paul Michael," I hear you saying. If my body is hungrily searching around for some fuel to burn, how come you said I'm not supposed to get hungry on your diet? Don't worry. The other secret is protein. Meat, as I said is really the basic food for human beings. Protein is what the body needs to replenish itself, rebuild tissues, replace old cells, and protein is what the body is smart about. Your system will use only the protein it requires and leave the rest, no matter how much you eat. But here's what I found out when I was looking for a way to lose weight. The body can't use proteins to make deposits in the "fat bank." Not unless there's nothing else at all in your system including body fat. That's what I meant when I said your body is smarter about proteins than about carbohydrates. And that's why you can eat all the pure proteins you want and still lose weight.

On my diet program you can eat all you want! All the protein (meat, fish, cheese, chicken, eggs) all the fats (butter, mayonnaise, heavy cream) but not all the starch you want. That's really the only gimmick. You must restrict (not completely cut out) your carbohydrate intake. That means you have to educate your mind as well as your metabolism about the contents of various foods. This report contains a chart you can refer to and a simplified list of allowable foods. At first, you'll have to look everything up. But after a while, when you've absorbed the principle, you'll rarely have to refer to any charts.

PAUL MICHAEL WEIGHT-LOSS TIP #2 <u>DON'T LET YOURSELF GO HUNGRY</u>. Most diets flounder on lack of willpower. For my diet, you don't need willpower. Abstinence is positively a drawback in this program. It was my own pitifully small willpower that led me to formulate my diet in the first place. Now this idea is a watchword with me. If losing weight depended on being able to endure hunger, I'd still be fat. Chances are that's true about you, too. So make up your mind that you won't <u>allow</u> yourself to be hungry. It's one of the rules! But make up your mind, too, that you're going to make a big change in the kinds of things you fill up on. If you're used to thinking of a "snack" as maybe a cookie or a little open-faced sandwich, start thinking of it as a nice slice of meat instead. Believe me, once you get used to it, it's every bit as satisfying, maybe even more. If you're worried that no diet that allows you to feel satisfied could work, don't worry. All you have to do is look at my wedding photo and look at me today to know it works.

What about all the fat in the Paul Michael diet? Okay, protein won't be stored as fat, but how can you actually take in pure fat and not put on pounds? Well, I have a theory, and my friend the biochemist has a theory. We both agree that it's so, because we've observed it in our own lives. Here are two of the reasons it works, maybe science will find more in the years to come. First, fat seems to satisfy better than any other food. In a way your body tends to be "smart" about fat, too. Anyway, that's what I think. Haven't you noticed that if you eat a piece of bread with butter it fills you up a lot quicker than bread alone? To put it another way, imagine eating a whole loaf of bread. You can en- vision it probably, without too much trouble. Now try to picture yourself eating a whole pound of butter. Disgusting isn't it? A little fat goes a long way. That's why I say, eat all the fat you want. Because I know you won't want as much butter as you want cake or pie or fruit. We human beings just aren't built that way.

What's the scientific explanation? The way my friend ex- plains it, fats can't be properly stored in the body without the help of some carbohydrates. If your intake of carbohydrates is very low, some of the fat will pass right through your system without being broken down and stored in adipose tissue. In a way, you're blocking the pathway that allows the body to make fatty tissue. Whatever the reasons, my diet plan allows you to reverse the old diet adages that forbid egg yolk, butter, hard cheese, hollandaise sauce, all the things you love. On the Paul Michael diet, fat is good!

PAUL MICHAEL WEIGHT-LOSS TIP #3 CHANGE YOUR WAY OF EATING TO CHANGE YOUR SHAPE. My plan is really a program for a change of lifestyle. This isn't a short-term quick weight loss diet, although you certainly will take off excess poundage fast. The low carbohydrate-high protein regimen is so easy and so satisfying that you can, and should, stay on it forever. This diet, with variations, naturally, is the way thin people live all the time! When you're a thin person, this is how you'll live, too.

Before you get all excited, let me hasten to explain what I don't mean when I say my diet is for the rest of your life. I don't mean that you can never eat another candy bar or piece of pie. I don't mean that you can't go back to your half grapefruit every day once the fat is gone. On the contrary. I found out from bitter experience that denying yourself that "forbidden" food you crave will only lead to an inner rebellion and ultimately to weight gain. But once you've experienced the energy, the sense of well-being, and the satisfaction that comes from following a low-carbohydrate program, your old, unhealthy eating patterns will be broken. Every week you stay on my diet is another step in re-educating your body to greater energy, better eating, and thinness. Even though it's a long-term plan, my diet is no life sentence: it's a full pardon from the curse of being overweight.

HOW THE DIET WORKS

The first question you're bound to ask after reading this or any other diet plan is, "how much weight can I expect to lose?" Of course, I can't predict exactly. I don't know how tall or how active you are or how much overweight. I can only tell you about my experience and that of my friends. When I started my diet, I weighed 260 pounds. For the first two weeks, I lost five pounds a week. The third week, I lost only about a pound, and I started thinking it was time to get back to the old drawing board. But then, in week four, I lost three pounds. After that, with a few more "plateaus" I kept right on losing. Today I weigh 174 pounds. Two years after the end of my diet.

My wife's story is different. When she started the diet, after seeing my success, she lost five pounds the first week. But the second week her total loss was only about a pound and a half. The third week was also slow. For a while we were puzzled about why the diet seemed to work better for me. Then it dawned on me. My wife weighed 140 pounds to start with. Her goal was only to lose about 20 pounds. Naturally it was easier for me, with so much excess fat, to take off pounds faster. But she was already much closer to her goal in these weeks than I was. She stuck to the diet and lost her 20 pounds in about nine weeks. And the marvel is we've both stayed slim over two years.

After I worked out my diet plan by trial and error, I decided to talk to some doctor friends about just why it seemed to work where others didn't. Medical men can't seem to agree on anything except after a long argument. One of my friends, Dr. S., insisted that the only way to lose weight was with the traditional "well-balanced" diet. Meaning you eat a little (very little) of everything, including breads, fruits, and sugars every day. "But look at me," I said. "I'm a living example that you're wrong." Fortunately, our other friend, Dr. F., came to my defense. "Of course, you're wrong," he said, "you know as well as I do that there's no proven dietary requirement for carbohydrates."

Well, they argued, and I listened ... What I learned is that some doctors are afraid of my low-carbohydrate diet because of a condition called ketosis. Ketosis, it seems, is associated with many serious diseases, such as acidosis and diabetes. But ketosis, as Dr. F. pointed out, is not itself a disease. In fact when I started doing research for this report, I discovered that just about the only study ever done with a diet so carbohydrate poor as to cause ketosis was done as a <u>cure</u>. The researchers had found that being slightly ketotic helped some epileptics. No harmful side effects were seen in that study.

What is ketosis? To put it simply, it's a sloughing off of partially digested foods. It happens with very low-carbohydrate diets because the body can't properly assimilate certain nutrients, mostly fats, without a little carbohydrate. Therefore, the unassimilated particles, called <u>ketone bodies</u> are given off, in the urine and in the breath.

As I listened to these discussions, I started to wonder whether my diet produced ketosis. It turns out there's a very simple way to find out. Little paper testing sticks, sold in drugstores under the name Keto-Stix, can be used to test the urine. I bought some, and tried it out. You know what I found? It's really almost impossible to get yourself into ketosis. At 60 grams a day, there was no trace of ketone bodies. Even at 30 grams a day I wasn't ketotic. Finally, by cutting back to almost zero carbohydrates, I managed to go into ketosis, for one day. But the next morning, I had a teaspoon of sugar in my coffee and bam. Back to normal. My personal conclusion is that ketosis is

nothing to worry about in the 30-60 gram range. Dr. F. still
says that ketosis is nothing to worry about anyway, as long as it
isn't severe or associated with any disease. By all means
consult your doctor while you're on my diet. By all means test your
urine to see if you're ketotic. My guess is you won't be and you'll
lose weight like crazy, too.

Once I got interested in the medical and scientific reasons
why my new diet works, I couldn't stop exploring. I've already
spoken of the satisfaction factor. Fats and proteins are just
so much more <u>filling</u> than other foods. I discovered an interesting scientific concept called the "appestat." It's something
like a thermostat in theory, only it controls your appetite.
Numerous experiments have shown that most obese people have broken
appestats. Fat folks eat because it's time to eat or because
they like the looks of the food or because they're depressed or
any one of a zillion other reasons that have nothing to do with
<u>hunger</u>. They don't even know what it feels like to be hungry. My
personal theory is that the low carbohydrate diet somehow restores
the appestat. That people may not know when to stop eating
carbohydrates, but with proteins and fats, they seem to regain
the ability to know when they've had enough. That's the reason
I think the diet works, and that's the reason it changes not only
your shirt size, but your way of life.

Here's something else I ran across in my reading. The body
burns carbohydrates a lot more efficiently than it does fats.
From the point of view of the fat man, that's bad. It means that
when you eat carbohydrates, your system squeezes every drop of

potential fat out of the food and piles it right on to your waistline. Not so with fat. About 10-15 per cent of the fat you eat can be excreted. In other words, it goes right through your body without being turned into extra pounds. Doctors call this the "thermic effect," or "specific dynamic action." I call it a terrific boon to unscientific fatties like me who just want to lose weight without losing our minds.

Because my diet lets you eat all the rich (i.e. fatty) foods you want, you don't feel deprived. How can you feel sorry for yourself when you're dining on cold salmon with mayonnaise sauce? And what about those heavenly bacon-and-egg breakfasts? Nobody would believe you're on a diet, and it's all because of the satisfying properties of fats and oils.

Another thing I believe is that a diet rich in fats and oils actually reduces craving for sweets. After a big steak smothered in onions or two whopping cheeseburgers, you're really <u>full</u>. I can't explain why, but it's a different kind of full from the way you feel after a big starchy dinner when you suddenly have to have a chocolate bar. Know the feeling? I certainly do, although it's only a memory now. Since I discovered my diet plan, I really don't get those irrational cravings any more. Call it the satisfaction factor or the appestat or whatever you like, I know it works for me, and I know it'll work for you.

Since this diet actually re-educates your body chemistry, it's wise to consult your doctor before you start my diet, or anyone's diet, for that matter. This is especially true if you're now taking any medication, have a history of disease, pregnant, or have any reason at all to suspect medical complications. Personally, I don't see my diet as an extreme measure or a health risk in any way. But I don't know you or your personal medical history, so check with your physician to be sure.

YOU ARE WHAT YOU EAT OR A ROLL IS A ROLL IS A ROLL

Now that you know the general simple plan of my Paul Michael Diet, let's get down to specifics. By now you know that the idea is to eat lots of protein and fat, very little carbohydrate. But how do these general categories break down into the actual foods we eat every day?

Proteins. Proteins are compounds made of specific sequences of amino acids. These acids are absolutely essential for cell growth. That's what doctors mean when they say proteins are the "building blocks" of the body. You can live for a while without proteins, but finally, the tissues will be unable to rebuild and repair themselves, and you'll die. In many parts of the world, it's hard for people to get enough protein. But here in the United States, we're lucky enough to have a protein-rich diet. We're affluent enough to literally live on protein. And, in fact, that's just what my diet plan suggests that you do. Where are proteins found? In meat, mainly. That means beef, poultry, fish, lamb, venison, rabbit, organ meats, any of the animals bred or hunted for meat. Protein foods also include eggs, cheese and milk (the more butterfat, the better, for this diet). Protein is also found, though somewhat less perfectly, in nuts, dried peas and beans, soybeans, even wheat. But vegetable proteins are not included in the foods you can eat in unlimited quantities. That's because in beans or wheat, even in nuts, the proteins are combined with carbohydrates. On this diet, the "yes" foods are meats (except processed meats such as hot dogs and sausages that contain carbohydrates) fish, chicken and turkey, eggs, cheese, milk and cream.

Fats. Everybody can recognize fats, of course. Fat is greasy or oily, just as the name implies. Fat is found in meat, (not much in fish) cheese and cream. Butter and salad dressing are almost pure fat. My program allows all these fatty substances you want. What about cholesterol? Well, I happen to believe from the research I've done, that too much starch has more to do with heart disease than too much fat, even saturated fat. But if you're worried about cholesterol, my diet certainly doesn't compel you to eat it. Generally speaking, the solid fats (butter, lard, meat fat) are the ones high in saturates, while liquid fats (oils) are the ones with the large percentage of polyunsaturates. Most medical people now agree that too much saturated fat contributes to high cholesterol in the blood. Just how much high cholesterol has to do with heart attacks is open to debate. But if it worries you, steer away from solid fats and stick to salad dressigns and marinades made with oils. (Olive oil, by the way, has the highest percentage of unsaturated fats among all the vegetable oils, in spite of claims on the labels of safflower oil products.)

Here's what you're allowed to eat freely on my diet: mayonnaise, butter, oils, shortening and margarine. Also included, of course, are the fats contained in beef, pork, lamb, chicken, cheese and cream, including the oil from canned seafood.

Carbohydrates. Now we come to the most important diet rule of all. PAUL MICHAEL WEIGHT-LOSS TIP #4 LIMIT YOUR CARBOHYDRATE INTAKE TO 60 GRAMS A DAY. To do it, you'll need a carbohydrate gram counter, at least at first. You'll find a partial one in the back of the book, but more complete lists are available in the form of inexpensive paperback books. Please understand I don't mean that if you go over 60 grams in a day the diet will be ruined. But 60 grams is a reasonable figure that you can stick with even through the tough situations like eating out with friends or going on vacation. If you can eat less, fine. A few days with no carbohydrates at all won't hurt you a bit, and the weight loss will be that much faster. The basic idea is to keep your intake at an average of no more than 60 grams per day.

What are carbohydrates? In ordinary language, they're starches. That means sugars, such as fruit sugar and refined sugar, plus the starches in grain, potatoes, fruits and vegetables. If you're used to thinking about calories instead of carbohydrates, you may be in for a few surprises about what are and are not diet foods according to this program. Grapefruit, for example, so dear to the hearts of most old-style dieters, is a severely restricted food on my plan. By the same token, you've already seen that old-style forbiddens like butter and mayonnaise are not only allowed, but recommended on my diet. Until you become accustomed to this new way of measuring the "diet power" of foods, it's best to look up everything you eat or plan to eat. Pure fats and proteins, of course, are mostly carbohydrate free. But watch out!

What about prepared salad dressings? If the label mentions sugar, you'll have at least a few grams of carbohydrate to add to your daily total.

As with most diets, it helps if you prepare meals for yourself. If you or your spouse dress the salad, you'll know for sure there's no hidden sugar. It's sometimes very hard to tell whether restaurant food contains hidden carbohydrates. That sauce, was it made with egg yolks (yea!) or with flour? (boo!) Could that tasty cheese dip possibly contain processed cheese spread (carbohydrates) instead of natural cheddar (almost none)? But as you become more practiced at estimating grams, you'll learn, too, what to order when eating out and what to avoid. And remember, nutrition, like most things related to the body, is an averaging process. If you went a little over the top in carbohydrates on Monday, cut way back on Tuesday. Will it hurt you to cut down to zero in carbohydrates? Surely not for one day. My guess is that you could go much longer in perfect health without letting one gram cross your lips.

To help take the strangeness out of carbohydrate gram counting, here's my special list of unlimited foods. Eat as much and as many of these as you feel like having. As time goes by, you'll find others.

FREE FOODS

(Zero or near-zero carbohydrates)

Anchovies
Anchovy pasta
Artificial sweetners

Bacon
Beef (All cuts, no prepared meatballs)
Beef broth or bouillon
Butter
Brains
Brandy
Caviar
Chicken
Chicken broth or bouillon
Corned beef
Cornish game hen
Coffee
Crabmeat
Duck
Eggs
Fat (Meat, bacon, etc.)
Fish
Gelatin (Plain or artificially sweetened)
Gin
Gizzard (Chicken or duck)
Goose
Ham
Hamburger
Head Cheese
Heart (Beef or mutton)
Kidneys
Lamb
Liver (Chicken, beef, other)
Lobster
Margarine
Mutton
Oils (all kinds)
Pork
Rum
Rye
Salmon
Salt
Sausage (Ground, not prepared with sugar or filler)
Sardines
Scotch
Shrimp
Spices (Any that contain no sugar)
Squab
Tea
Tongue
Tripe
Tuna
Turkey
Veal
Venison
Vodka
Whiskey

These are some of the foods you can eat in <u>unlimited</u> quantities.

But there are lots more that contain so little carbohydrate that you'd have to eat an abnormal amount to make any significant difference. Since my diet is a <u>low</u> carbohydrate plan, rather than a <u>no</u> carbohydrate plan, I've made up a list for you of things you can eat <u>in moderation</u> every day, and still lose weight.

<u>Moderation Foods</u>
(low in carbohydrates)

Asparagus
Avocado
Bean Sprouts
Cabbage
Cauliflower
Celery
Chicory
Chives
Cucumber
Eggplant
Endive
Escarole
Fennel
Kale
Lettuce
Mushrooms
Okra
Olives
Onions
Parsley
Peppers
Pickles (not sweet)
Pumpkin (unsweetened)
Radishes
Rhubarb
Sauerkraut
Scallions
Spinach
String Beans
Summer squash
Tomatoes
Watercress
Wax beans
Zucchini

With a little ingenuity, you'll be able to devise substitutes in all your recipes. Try stuffing a chicken with chopped spinach mixed with egg and spices, for example. The only limit is your imagination. Lettuce or cucumber slices can substitute for crackers to dunk in formerly forbidden dips. (Confess, it was really the dip you were interested in all along, wasn't it?) I could go on and on, but you'll soon see for yourself. My diet allows you so many good things you won't even miss starch and sugar after a while.

What about "forbidden" foods? As I've said, never deprive yourself. If you love to have a glass of sherry before dinner, go ahead. Just make sure you save up enough carbohydrate credits so you don't go above 60. Even ice cream or chocolate candy isn't forbidden if you plan it into your diet. But there are foods that contain so many carbohydrates that they leave you almost no margin for error in the rest of your eating. Here's a list of what I call:

WATCH-OUT-FOODS

Bananas	Candy	Corn
Bread	Cereals	Cornstarch
Cake	Cookies	Crackers
Dates	Macaroni	Rice
Dried beans	Milk	Spaghetti
Figs	Pancakes	Sugar
Flour	Pasta	Syrup
Fruits, fresh and dried	Peas	
Honey	Potatoes, white or sweet	
Jam	Raisins	

PAUL MICHAEL WEIGHT-LOSS TIP # 5   EAT SIX MEALS A DAY. When I started developing this diet the hardest thing for me to do was to convince people to eat six meals a day. They had been taught since childhood that extra meals meant extra weight. The facts are that just the opposite is true. Let me explain why three meals are really a mistake. You are conditioned to eating meals at set times. Yet frequently you are so hungry when the next meal arrives you <u>overeat</u>. Sometimes to compensate for this people will have little snacks. However, the snack actually piles on more weight than two full size meals.

Here's how the process works. I guess I can use myself as the best example. When I would go on a traditional type diet I would try to cut out calories. I would eat the prescribed 2 ounces of lean beef and the cup of clear chicken broth. However, an hour later I was hungry again. Maybe later I would "sneak" a piece of pie. However, I never really counted the pie as a meal.

Now, my plan is to <u>count every time you eat as a regular meal</u>. In the second part of this report (psychological section) I tell you to only eat when you are hungry. Chances are you'll be hungry a half-dozen times a day. As you are not locked into three meals at prescribed times you'll find you actually will eat less! This is the very point: Eating six meals a day will give you less weight adding food than three meals a day. You may find this hard to believe. Try it and you'll understand how it works.

It is, of course, important for you to understand that these six meals must follow the low carbohydrate plan outlined. It's <u>not</u> going to help you to eat six meals that look like this:

>Orange juice & danish (1st)
>Milk and toast (2nd)
>Hero Sandwich (3rd)
>Beer and pizza (4th)
>Lasagna (5th)
>Noodle Soup, Sandwich, Ice Cream (6th)

What I am saying is that you should plan your meals to include high protein and low carbohydrates. These extra meals will actually help in your weight loss plan .. as hard as that is to believe!

A natural question is how does a person eat six meals. Well, this can be broken up into any way you find convenient. The plan can take any form that you find convenient to your schedule and eating likes and dislikes. Again, see the psychological section for some guidelines. Some people (who retire early) may be eating their second supper at 9 p.m. while for others that may come at 2 a.m. However, here is a fairly typical schedule for someone following my diet plan:

Breakfast #1	6 a.m.
Breakfast #2	10 a.m.
Lunch #1	1 p.m.
Lunch #2	4 p.m.
Dinner #1	8 p.m.
Supper #1	11 p.m.

You may ask what are differences in meal planning. Well, essentially what you are doing is taking what you now eat and splitting it into two meals. Or I should say what you would eat on the new diet you are about to begin and splitting it into two meals. You might make some variations. For example, here are two ways to approach your new diet at breakfast:

APPROACH #1	Breakfast:	3 eggs 6 slices of bacon
APPROACH #2	Breakfast #1:	2 eggs 3 slices of bacon
	Breakfast #2:	1 egg 3 slices of bacon

The obvious comment is how can this help as the same amount of food is being consumed. Interestingly, it helps for a variety of reasons. First, you are less likely to be hungry if you spread out your meals. This is all important in any sound diet plan. Second, you are getting food into your system as your body can use it. This is less taxing on your system. When large meals are consumed your digestive system is literally overwhelmed and unable to cope with all the food. To understand this principle just think back to how you felt after your last Thanksgiving dinner. We all know that bloated feeling. It's not only difficult to work but you know the physical strain on your body. Before you write this portion of the report off as a wild idea think for a moment. Most of the inhabitants of the earth eat just this way. Think of all the animals, birds, and mammals you've seen in zoos, in parks and in the country. They know what's good for their system. Do they sit down to three square meals a day? Of course not. They eat six, nine, or nineteen meals a day. Interestingly, scientists recently have conducted experiments in which animals were allowed to eat only twice daily. Guess the result ... they grew fat though eating a perfectly formulated diet!

PAUL MICHAEL WEIGHT-LOSS TIP #6   NEVER DEPRIVE YOURSELF OF FOOD. An important part of this diet is NEVER do without food. To be specific you will not lose weight by depriving your body of food. This report tells you which foods to cut out. However, under no circumstances should you try to lose weight by fasting for a day or skipping meals. On the one hand, don't eat if you're not hungry. However, most important is that you can not get thin by depriving yourself! The secret is to make sure you are eating the RIGHT type of foods. You, your cells, your stomach should be satisfied. One of the reasons traditional diets fail is that they are built on eating less of the wrong foods rather than more of the right foods.

PAUL MICHAEL WEIGHT-LOSS TIP #7   COUNT CARBOHYDRATES AT EVERY MEAL. One of the places we all fall down is staring tomorrow or believing that a little mistake can't hurt. In the beginning it will take constant attention to make the diet work. The one place I noticed the biggest problem is when individuals don't count every eating as a meal. For example, walking by a tray of dried fruits may have you reach for a seemingly meaningless snack. However, a half dozen little prunes contain 80 grams of carbohydrates ... more than your allowance for a whole day! In the menu section I outline some low (or no) carbohydrate menus. To show you how easy it is for you to get off base it is worthwhile for you to consider your carbohydrate count for yesterday. What did you really eat? What did it really cost you in carbohydrates? The last time I went off this diet (to any real extent) was when I had dinner at a friend's house. Take a look at what happened:

Christmas Eggnog (8 oz.)	Grams	36.00
Glass of Beer		10.6
Spaghetti & Meatballs		104.00
Ear of Corn		21.0
Orange Sherbert		30.8

You'll notice it was almost a 200 gram dinner. What's most important, I didn't really enjoy it that much. A zero gram highball would really have pleased me just as much as a thirty-six gram glass of eggnog. The point of all this? Watch out for traps.

If you are going to go off your diet plan to do it for something that you'll really enjoy. It's all too easy to slip if you're not careful. However, if you are watching out it's easy as pie (I should say beef) to stay on target.

SUGGESTED MENUS

There is never any reason for you to be bored with this diet plan. You are only limited by your imagination. There is no end to interesting dishes for your six meals. All it takes is a little creative thinking and a little planning. Below are a number of meals my wife has produced in recent weeks. To create your own simply sit down with your carbohydrate gram counter and plan new combinations of foods.

BREAKFAST

I like to start the day with a hearty breakfast. It's really quite easy to do without pancakes and syrup. In fact, I feel good (and ready to go) rather than logged down after one of these breakfasts:

          Scrambled eggs with sour cream and caviar
          Herb Omelette
          Eggs Benedict (without the muffins)
          Meat Buffet (ham, sausage, and hamburger)
          Eggs with lox/salami/bacon/cheese/shrimp

LUNCH

Lunch offers an unlimited opportunity to explore new taste ideas that you've long forgotten. The fact is the sandwich became a way for me to fill up rather than a taste experience. Remember salads? Give some thought to the chef salad and its interesting varieties. Tuna, Chicken, Crab, Lobster, Turkey, and Bacon make great salads.

Breadless sandwiches are a tasty experience. Here's a few of the limitless possibilities:

A) Put two slices of ham and sprigs of watercress between two slices of squared off swiss cheese.

B) Using a large cucumber of Zucchini make mini-open sandwiches. Simply use the vegetable to replace the bread. Cover with tuna, shrimp or lobster.

C) The Cucumber Boat. Slice off the top of a cucumber, hollow out removing the seeds and stuff with any meat or fish salad.

D) Green Pepper Bell Ringer. Simply hollow out a green pepper and do the same. Also try celery stalks, lettuce leaves and if you're lucky enough to find fenucci at your local supermarket use that.

Also give some thought to that all American favorite the hamburger and the many and varied ways it can be prepared. Of course there is no rule against using traditional dinner dishes at lunch.

DINNER/SUPPER

My favorite dinners are all those that I thought I couldn't eat because they just weren't for people who were dieting. Just a few suggestions:

A) Scallops in butter and garlic sauce
B) Coq au vin
C) Broiled lobster with melted butter

D) Barbecued spareribs
E) Flounder stuffed with crabmeat
F) Veal Piccata

You may say these entrees are fine but what about entire meals. To give you an idea of how simple this plan is I've listed my meals for yesterday and their actual gram count. These are only an example but they should give you an insight.

Breakfast #1
Two eggs	0.0
Six strips of bacon	0.0
Coffee with cream	0.2

Breakfast #2
One egg	0.0
Tea with lemon	0.0

Lunch #1
Green salad w/dress	6.5
Steak	0.0
Diet soda	0.0

Lunch #2
Highball	0.0
Tuna salad	0.0
Coffee with cream	0.2

Dinner #1
Sauterne wine dry	4.0
Hamburger	0.0
Broccoli w/hollandaise	4.7
Diet Gelatin	0.0
Tea	0.0

Dinner #2
Chicken broth	0.0
Slice Whole Wheat Bread	11.0
Two pats butter	0.0
Left over tuna salad	0.0

You'll notice that my total carbohydrate count for the day was less than thirty; yet I certainly didn't starve myself. If for example one day I went on a binge and had two pieces of custard pie (35 grams each) the next day I'd cut down to almost zero grams of carbohydrates with a diet that looks like this:

Breakfast #1
Three eggs
Bacon
Black Coffee

Breakfast #2
One soft boiled egg

Lunch #1
Tuna Salad
Cottage Cheese
D-Zerta Gelatin
Sugar-free Diet Soda

Lunch #2
Two large hamburger patties

Dinner #1
Highball
Steak
Large Salad

Supper #1
12 Spareribs

Entire day gram count ... (0)

Breakfast #1
Hamburger pattie
2 eggs fried in butter
Black Coffee

Breakfast #2
Bacon
Coffee

Lunch #1
Filet of Sole, lemon butter sauce
Salad
Tea or Coffee

Lunch #2
Chicken Salad with mayonnaise
Diet soda

Dinner #1
Antipasta (salami, green peppers, anchovies,
          prosciutto, cheese)
Pot roast
Cottage Cheese
Tea

<u>Dinner #2</u>
Steak
Salad
Tea
Large wedge of Swiss cheese

Here are some specific recipes that show you how planning or substitution make implementing this new diet easy. You'll note they all have less than one gram of carbohydrates per serving and yet are quite interesting.

<u>SUPER EGG DROP SOUP</u>

2 pints chicken soup
2 eggs

Heat soup to boiling. Beat eggs and drop into broth, a little at a time. Stir well. Simmer 3 minutes.

<u>SCALLOPS IN GARLIC BUTTER</u>

½ lb. scallops
1 lemon
¼ stick butter
2 cloves of garlic (crushed)

Melt butter in broiler pan. Add scallops. Sprinkle evenly with crushed garlic. Broil 5-10 minutes.

<u>LUSTY LONDON BROIL</u>

2 Tbsp. Grated Parmesan cheese
4 Tbsp. olive oil
2 Tbsp. tarragon vinegar
1 tsp. salt
3 lbs. London Broil

Mix cheese, oil, vinegar and salt. Place meat in mixture. Marinate overnight, then broil.

<u>MUSSELS MARINIERE</u>

5 lbs. mussels
3 onions cut in quarters
salt and ground pepper
2 cups dry white wine
4 Tbsp. butter
2 bay leaves
1 tsp. thyme

Wash outside mussel shells. Place mussels and all ingredients in covered deep pot. Bring to boil and then simmer for 10 minutes.

LEG OF LAMB WITH MUSTARD SAUCE

½ cup of French-type mustard
2 Tbsp. Worcestershire sauce
1 clove crushed garlic
1 tsp. sweet basil
¼ tsp. ginger powder
2 Tbsp. olive oil
6 lb. leg of lamb

Blend ingredients and then beat by hand to make a creamy sauce. Spread over lamb a few hours before you put in oven. Roast 350° 1-1¼ hours.

SHRIMP IN GARLIC BUTTER

4 lbs. shrimp with shells
½ lb. butter
2-3 garlic cloves (crushed)
¼ cup chopped parsley
¼ cup dry sherry

Cream butter with garlic. Add everything else with dash Worcestershire sauce, and nutmeg. Cook shrimp separately by boiling water; then adding shrimp; then shutting off when water returns to boil; then let sit for 1 minute; then remove shrimp. Dot creamed ingredients over shrimp in buttered dish. Bake for 20 minutes in 425° oven.

STEAK AU POIVRE

Salt
1 Tbsp. cognac
1 tsp. coarsely crushed white peppercorns (mortar & pestle)
¼ cup heavy cream
½ tsp. Dijon mustard
3/4 inch thick steak (filet)

Pan fry steak in 1 Tbsp. butter until cooked to the way you like it (rare, medium, well). Transfer to warm platter and cover with foil to keep warm. Add cognac to frying pan. Heat and stir. Add crushed pepper and cream and bring to simmer, stirring. Stir in mustard and pour over steak.

FILET OF SOLE WITH CREAM SAUCE

1½ lbs. filet
1 cup dry white wine
1 shallot

Tbsp. butter
2 egg yolks
½ cup heavy cream
1 tsp. parsley (chopped)

Spread sole in shallow baking dish. Add wine, salt and
pepper and sprinkle with chopped shallot. Dot fish with
butter and bake at 350° for 20 minutes or until cooked
but still firm. Drain off liquid from baking dish and
simmer down to 1 cup. Mix 2 egg yolks with cream and
stir carefully into reduced fish stock. Add 1 tsp. of
chopped parsley. Pour sauce over filets and glaze brief-
ly under hot broiler.

ROAST LAMB WITH SAUSAGE

6 lb. leg of lamb, boned, rolled and stuffed with ½ lb.
            sausage (have your butcher do this
            for you)
1 cup chicken broth (made from bouillon)
salt
pepper

Season lamb with salt and pepper and roast in shallow
roasting pan, uncovered, for 30 minutes. Turn so that
lamb is brown on all sides. Turn oven down to 300° and
cook 45 minutes more. During the last 15 minutes add
broth. For pink meat (roast 1¼ hours) for brown (roast
1½ hours). Remove lamb and place on platter. Scrape
sides of pan, mixing with juices. Season to taste and
strain into a gravy boat. Use to spoon over carved lamb.

TARRAGON CHICKEN

6 med. chicken breasts
salt
pepper
1 lemon
2 Tbsp. butter plus 1 stick of butter
1 tsp. dried tarragon
1 tbsp. Beau Monde Seasoning

Cut lemon and rub each piece of chicken with rind. Season
with salt, pepper and Beau Monde Seasoning. Place chicken
in shallow pan (skin side down) and dot with 2 Tbsp. butter. Brown lightly under broiler -- 5 minutes each side.
In a sauce pan, melt stick of butter with tarragon. Simmer for 10 minutes and pour over chicken. Turn broiler
heat to 350° and cook another 15 minutes. Serve with chopped parsley.

SALMON MOUSSE

1 envelope of non-flavored gelatin
½ slice of large onion
½ cup mayonnaise
1 tsp. dill seed
1 cup heavy cream
2 Tbsp. lemon juice
½ cup boiling water
¼ tsp. paprika
1 lb. can salmon

Blend gelatin, lemon juice, onion and water at high
speed for 40 seconds. Add mayonnaise, paprika, dill and
salmon. Blend 30 seconds. Add 1/3 cup cream. Blend
30 seconds. Add another 1/3 cup cream. Blend 30 seconds.
Add last 1/3 cup cream. Blend 30 seconds. Pour into
4 cup mold. Refrigerate.

CHICKEN SUPREME

2 chicken breasts skinned and boned
½ stick butter
lemon
salt
pepper
¼ cup chicken broth (made from bouillon)
¼ cup dry white wine
3/4 cup heavy cream

Squeeze lemon, salt and pepper on one side of chicken
breasts. Melt butter in casserole in 400° oven. When
butter is melted, take casserole out and place breasts,
seasoned side down in casserole. Turn oven to 375° and
cover casserole and cook chicken for 6-10 minutes.
Turn breasts over, season, and cook another 6 minutes
(covered). Take chicken out and put in warm dish and
cover with foil. Put casserole on top of stove with
melted butter sauce and add chicken bouillon and wine.
Stir with wooden spoon and boil down to 2-3 tablespoons.
Butter should burn a tiny bit. Then add cream and cook
until thick. Pour sauce over chicken and sprinkle with
parsley (chopped).

<u>PART II Psychological Aspects of Weight Loss</u>

I made a promise to you. I said you'd actually feel like

eating less. Well, part of the reason you eat a certain way has nothing to do with hunger. At least, that's the way it was for me. I ate when I was happy (to celebrate), I ate when I was depressed (to cheer me up), I ate thick soups in the winter (to warm up), I had tall cold soft drinks in the summer (to cool off). In fact, at the least little excuse I was off and eating. The fact of the matter is that heavy folks just plain eat more than thin folks. There's a famous experiment a psychologist I know told me about. He said a few years ago at an eastern university the following experiment was conducted. Outside of the school cafeteria students leaving from lunch were asked to participate in an "advertising experiment." They were to taste a cracker and rate the taste quality. They could taste as many as they liked before making the rating. Here's the interesting fact. Overweight students ate an average of $9\frac{1}{4}$ crackers before making the rating. Thin students ate an average of $1\frac{1}{4}$ crackers before making the rating. What's more, all the tasters had just finished lunch! Some of us, you see, are just in the habit of eating. This brings us to PAUL MICHAEL WEIGHT-LOSS TIP #8   ASK YOURSELF THE NEXT TIME YOU ARE ABOUT TO EAT IF YOU ARE REALLY HUNGRY ... IF THE ANSWER IS NO HAVE A GLASS OF WATER INSTEAD. I can't tell you how many times I went through this little experiment and how much weight it really saved me. I'd guess at least 35 pounds. It might be worth looking at why we eat when we are not hungry so we can better understand ourselves.

Unfortunately, there are a lot of overweight people who, without realizing it, wish to be fat in order to present to the world a reason or excuse for their social inadequacies. Perhaps the fat individual wasn't accepted by his peer group as a teenager;

so, rather than admit to a personality flaw or to the possibility of being physically unappealing, he overate, becoming heavier and more and more unattractive. Finally he could say, "Nobody likes me because I'm so fat. If I wasn't fat, I would be popular." This is only one example among many for why some fat persons "need" to remain fat -- as a protection against society's possible rejection of them, for reasons other than being fat. It is easier to be rejected because of fatness than because of flaws in personality, intelligence or family/educational/cultural/ethnic background. For some people, maintaining their overweight condition prevents them from socializing, which they may have a great fear of, a dread that may stem from childhood experiences. Some unmarried women use obesity as an escape from male attention, thus relieving them of the necessity of making a decision to marry. Only by becoming aware of these sad reasons for being obese can you successfully adhere to a diet.

You can never really get rid of your childhood; you may be able to scrutinize what you absorbed incidentally and overtly as a child, you may be able to ascertain whether you are suffering from excess weight because of specific family experiences, and you may even be able to cope with any insight into yourself ... but childhood experiences are forever intertwined in the make-up of your personality traits, behavior patterns, emotional reactions, and your eating habits. For example, if as a child your mother presented you with a treat, be it candy, cake or ice-cream, each time you were especially good and cooperative, or if this goody represented a pacifier to console you when you cried or were unhappy, then there is a good chance you transferred this need for a sweet, when unhappy, tense or frustrated, into your adult years. The patterns of behavior set in childhood are unconsciously and unwittingly carried over into your adulthood.

Knowing all this doesn't take off pounds but it does help you understand. Understanding does lead to taking off pounds. For example I thought about my childhood and found an interesting fact that has now saved me lots of weight. When I was a child my mother always said to me, "Finish what's on your plate, the children in Europe are starving." In fact when I got to Europe on my first vacation the first thing I did was look for the starving children. It wasn't until I was grown up that I realized that finishing what's on my plate couldn't help the starving children. (It only meant I'd get fatter while they stayed hungry.) A psychologist said I was still trying to win my mother's approval by finishing everything on my plate. I noticed thin folks leave food on their plate. By doing the same I started to lose weight. PAUL MICHAEL WEIGHT-LOSS TIP #9   ALWAYS LEAVE SOMETHING ON YOUR PLATE AT THE END OF EACH MEAL. Mothers often feed their babies regardless of whether or not baby is hungry. If the body requires food, the central and autonomous nervous systems and certain muscles signal the brain that hunger is present. If you eat even when hunger doesn't call, merely appetite calls, then you are conditioned to eat at any time and filling the body with food that the body cells do not require results in fatness. Because mother always fed you, ignoring your body's needs, does not mean that you have to continue this conditioned habit. A parent may have experienced

poverty in his youth and because he or she was deprived
of food, he will, unconsciously, almost force feed his
children, hoping, therefore to give them everything. When eating gets out of control, you can be sure it isn't because you
are hungry.

The act of chewing, of moving the mouth, is pleasurable for
the majority of human beings. Newborns and infants are wholly
involved in the act of oral gratification; their need to suck, to
mouth anything, almost continually, is inherent and normal -- in
babies. When this constant desire to have something in your
mouth is carried over into adolescent and post adolescent years,
then you should stop and analyze why your desire to chew is so
strong. (Smoking is another answer for those who need to be continually oral.) If chewing is a pleasurable part of your life and
you cannot or wish not to discontinue it, then substitute the
kinds of food you chew. I found that a lot of weight I put on
was simply that I wanted to have something to do with my mouth
while I was watching television. Initially I took up smoking
and lost thirty (count them thirty) pounds. Then the government
told me that's not good for me so I switched to sugarless gum.
Now when I'm watching TV I reach for sugarless gum. Since all I
want is mouth movement this is great. PAUL MICHAEL WEIGHT-LOSS
TIP #10   ALWAYS KEEP LOTS OF SUGARLESS GUM HANDY. This really
works. Keep your mouth going but at no calories. I have one
friend that said just by switching from slices of cheese and
bologna to carrot sticks (as a TV snack) he saves 8,000 calories a
week. That's a staggering 400,000 calories every year! That one

tip could really save you a few inches on your waistline.

Many housewives whose husbands are absent due to lengthy business trips and who, as a result, are lonely, seek food as a substitute for love and companionship. A lonely widow or un-married, unfulfilled young woman also can be caught in the un-thinking enslavement to food, in bulk, as a way to assuage the loneliness and as a way to be no longer alone (food is keeping you company). Men who are lonely bachelors, who are bored, who are widowers may indulge in making food the center of their lives for want of anything or anyone else in the center. Why do these people seek food instead of other people, other pursuits such as hobbies, sports or employment?

PAUL MICHAEL WEIGHT-LOSS TIP #11   <u>FIND OUT WHY YOU QUIT IN THE PAST</u>. Chances are this is not the first diet you've ever been on. The advantage of this diet is that it really works with-out a great deal of willpower. However, one of the ways I finally beat the diet syndrome is not with a knife and fork but with a paper and pencil. I want you to sit down now and gather up this extra psychological ammunition.

Here's all you do. Sit down with a paper and pencil and write down all the reasons you stopped dieting in the past. Probably you can come up with a pretty long list. Here are some typical reasons that I gave and friends of mine gave:

> I was hungry all the time.
>
> I went out to a restaurant and saw a piece of pie that I couldn't resist.
>
> The diet food was boring.

A client came to town and I had to take
him out to dinner.

My mother-in-law made ---- and I wanted to
eat it to please her.

This objective listing may be painful. Maybe you've
dieted ten, twenty, or two hundred times before. But one thing
you'll find; you always stopped for a reason. Identification of
that reason is a key to diet success.

Being armed with this information you can now use it to prevent it happening again. Certain reasons are taken care of by the
diet itself. For example, on this diet you simply won't be hungry.
On the other hand if you find you go off your diet everytime while
you are at a restaurant you can plan a strategic attack for deal-
ing with the problem. Knowing that restaurants are your downfall
you can plan for this. First, you can attempt to avoid restaurants that feature rich desserts. Second, you can order extra appetizers so when dessert comes around you're stuffed. And perhaps
even more important, know that if you slip up once it's not the
end of the world.

My experience is that first piece of pie leads to a second
which leads to an ice cream soda. Knowing that a little slip
doesn't make that much difference is very important. Frequently
people use a single mistake as an excuse to drop a diet plan.
Don't worry about losing a single battle; just worry about losing
the war.

The important part about this discussion is KNOW THYSELF.
By using the ammunition of knowing your "falling off point" in
advance you can deal with it and plan for it. Advance warnings

are easy to spot. All that's required is sitting down and honestly evaluating your past successes and failures! This little exercise can make all the difference.

PAUL MICHAEL WEIGHT-LOSS TIP # 12   CONVINCE YOURSELF THAT IT CAN BE DONE.   This diet tip, to some, may be the most important. Nineteen years before Christ, the poet Virgil wrote," ... they are able because they think they are able." There are any number of examples in our lives which prove we first must convince ourselves of a fact before we can accomplish it. For generations football coaches have been telling their players that they have to win in their heads before they can win out in the field.

The starting point must be for YOU to understand that YOU CAN LOSE WEIGHT. The facts are simple. Lots of people have lost weight. I lost almost a hundred pounds. All of the people that have lost weight are no different than you. But first you have to convince yourself that you can do it. Have you ever sat down and pictured yourself thin? I want you to take five minutes and imagine yourself at your desired weight. Imagine how you will look; how you will act. Picture the clothes you will wear. Now, hold this mental picture and consider it at least twice a day. Don't think of yourself in some vague form as being the desired weight; rather get a vivid picture of exactly how you will look. Imagine your wardrobe in its every detail. Having a mental picture of a successful new you helps achieve a successful diet. Take a few minutes every morning as you wake up to imagine yourself thin. This delightful picture of yourself will help keep you from eating that extra sweet you really shouldn't have.

PAUL MICHAEL WEIGHT-LOSS TIP #13   <u>MAKE EVERY MEAL AN EVENT</u>.

Let's face facts. Some meals offer satisfaction while other meals do not. Have you ever considered what goes into the meals that produce the most satisfaction? Interestingly, it's hardly ever the chemical composition of those meals. It is as easy to obtain satisfaction from a (low carbohydrate) tuna salad meal as from a (high carbohydrate) bean salad meal. What is important are things like who we ate with, where we ate, the quantity of food consumed.

You may wonder what point I'm getting at. Well, one of the reasons you are willing to pay more for a meal at Le Madrigal French Restaurant than at Joe's Diner has nothing to do with the quality of the food. At the fancy French restaurant they serve you on linen tablecloths with sterling silver tableware. At the beanery you eat at a plastic counter and they sling the food at you.

The point is simple. If you walk by the fridge and grab a hunk of swiss cheese and stuff it in your mouth it doesn't do much psychologically for you. On the other hand you can take that same piece of cheese, put it on a bed of lettuce, and eat it with a knife and fork. From the standpoint of calories, carbohydrates, and general food values both types of eating are the same. From the standpoint of food satisfaction we are looking at two totally different experiences.

Whatever I'm going to eat must always be served on a plate. This is one little tip I'm sure saved me ten pounds last year alone. Remember what I said, every time you eat it counts as a meal. Try making every meal an event. You'll find you get more out of exactly the same amount of food!

PAUL MICHAEL WEIGHT-LOSS TIP #14 GET STARTED WITHIN THE NEXT 48 HOURS. Have you ever noticed how deadline dates help you achieve your goals? Sure I'm writing this report to make money but I also sincerely want you to lose weight. Therefore I'm going to tell you where most diets (in fact most goals in life) break down. That, my friend, is the "I'll start next week" syndrome. Read this report and then reread it. But please make a mental pledge to yourself you'll start in the next 48 hours. One of the reasons I've kept this report short is so you could quickly read through it and get started.

Procrastination is one of the most human of emotions. I'll give you a personal example that happened to me some ten years ago before I developed this diet. Right after my anniversary (in October) I pledged to myself I was going to start a diet. Well, next thing you know it was Thanksgiving and no time to start. Then came Christmas and who can diet on the holidays? In January there was the usual round of office parties. In February I always take my winter vacation. In the interest of space I won't tell you how I created an alibi for each month that followed. On my next wedding anniversary I still hadn't made a move in the right direction. I think you get the point.

This diet is not only simple to follow but simple to act on. Make the pledge right now that you'll put it in action in the next 48 hours. Let me tell you from my own experience if you put it off longer than a week you probably won't get started.

And while you are creating deadline dates write down one other. I want you to write down, as an inspiration, what you want to weigh six months from today. Simply put down your weight today and what your six month goal is. Now lets get started on achieving it. You have the ammunition in the pages of this report.

PAUL MICHAEL WEIGHT-LOSS TIP #15 <u>PLEDGE TO YOURSELF DURING THE NEXT SIX MONTHS YOU'LL FIND A NEW HOBBY.</u> I took up bowling and started to lose pounds. Not only did the bowling give me less eating time but the fun exercise helped knock off weight. You may not believe this but I really think eating was my hobby. I'd look forward to big dinners and new restaurants the way a stamp collector looked forward to finding a new stamp. When I realized that eating was not really a very healthy hobby I was on my way to losing!

PAUL MICHAEL WEIGHT-LOSS TIP #16 <u>WHEN YOU ARE TIRED ... GO TO SLEEP NOT TO THE FRIDGE.</u> I found I gained most of my weight at night when other folks were actually sleeping.

When the body is fatigued, it needs sleep. Regrettably, most overweight people eat when they are tired. Why? A compulsion? A message from the body informs you that sleep is required; the fat person misconstrues this message, interprets the signal as one of hunger ... and thus eats. When you are tired, sleep; logically you cannot eat while you are sleeping. Fall into some kind of routine of sleeping and eating and do not deviate from it; there is, indeed, a time to eat and a time to sleep. The time to eat is when you are honestly hungry -- not when your appetite is awakened. Don't be a slave to your appetites. Free your mind of your conditioned and often pre-adolescent responses to food and follow your body's signals. Robots can be re-programmed and so can people with overweight problems.

PAUL MICHAEL WEIGHT-LOSS TIP #17 <u>ASK YOURSELF IF THE MEAL YOU ARE ABOUT TO HAVE IS A RESULT OF HUNGER OR HABIT.</u>

To use an old cliché, we are all creatures of habit, and this is why many people overeat. It's programming again or conditioning if you like that word. You may have had an adequate, filling breakfast, but at work, there is a 10:00 a.m. coffee break with doughnuts and Danish offered. Your appetite hungers for these goodies, even though your body cells are not requesting additional nourishment. Eating during the coffee break is a mind habit, not a body habit. You eat because you are there, not because you need or really desire the fattening accompaniments to your coffee. Habits are extremely difficult monsters to obliterate.

Perhaps you realize that you eat more than you should because you are a victim of improper food habits. Twelve noon in our culture indicates lunch time, eating time. Man's mechanical clocks tell you to consume food, but does your body "clock" signal you to eat? If you are not hungry at twelve noon, don't eat a meal (and if you are not at work and thus on a schedule, avoid eating until you are truly hungry and craving nutrition). Maybe just a salad or other light food that is not full of sugar and starch. Don't be tyrannized by mechanical clocks; eight, twelve, and six o'clock are not the correct eating times for everyone.

Your body's requirements for nourishment work on an individualized basis; eating automatically will surely accumulate extra pounds automatically. Just because you have always eaten delicatessen on Saturday night does not mean that you must continue this food habit. Or are you aware that you always consume certain foods simply because your family has always eaten them; are you cognizant of the fact that you may retain poor eating habits simply because you've always eaten that way ... an automatic response to the ingestion of too much foods, too much of the wrong kinds of foods, and eating at times during the day that were set as a result of convenience and not according to your body's needs.

PAUL MICHAEL WEIGHT-LOSS TIP #18 DON'T TELL ANYONE YOU'RE ON A DIET. This is true for many reasons. People fall into two categories. Those that tell you that you don't need to be on a diet and those that nag you to go on a diet. Neither is a help. Your eating plan should be yours and yours alone. Their seemingly good-natured interest just reminds you that you have a problem.

Overweight people eat too much, too often and eat too much sugar and starch ladened foods. The more friends and relatives bother you about your heaviness, the more you are apt to eat more, perhaps to show them that you are free to eat when you please and that their nagging will not control your habits. Another vicious cycle begins: your eating of excessive quantities of food leads you to an obese condition; a glance in the mirror reveals your unattractive state which in turn creates feelings of strong dislike in yourself. You may become immersed in self-depreciation which makes you want to seek consolation. The vicious cycle completes itself when you walk into the kitchen searching for food to soothe you in your depressed state. After you stuff yourself (even though you are not truly hungry), you probably feel guilty and quite displeased with yourself ... and so the cycle begins anew.

The only one you'll want to tell you are on a diet is your wife or husband. A mate can help by keeping food of the starchy and sweet nature out of the house. Their help can help you win the battle of the bulge.

PAUL MICHAEL WEIGHT-LOSS TIP #19 IF THERE IS A FOOD YOU LOVE DON'T CUT IT OUT OF YOUR DIET. Before you say that is the opposite of what I told you about avoiding sweets and starches read the tip again. It simply says if there is one food you love it probably won't hurt that much. My favorite food is pizza. Even though it's not on my diet plan I always have a slice every week. I soon realized that it was not the pizza that put pounds on me BUT rather the pizza in combination with chocolate, cheese-cake, toast, lasagna and fifty other low protein foods I ate. Denying yourself a favorite food does not make your desire go away. If anything the opposite is true. The following is a true case based on a cousin of mine.

Upon the onset of puberty, M. developed a severe case of acne. Her unsightly skin problem never receded during adolescence and if anything, her condition worsened. Various remedies in the form of ointments, creams and vitamins, were suggested by her two dermatologists. One of the doctors admonished her for eating chocolate, in any form, and forbade her to eat it ever again, for he determined that chocolate was the possible if not probable cause for her particular case of acne. All during her adolescent years she was not allowed to eat any foods that contained chocolate substances, no matter how small the amount. Her mother watched her very closely, making sure M. abided by the doctor's orders.

Her acne condition improved somewhat but her desire for chocolate never diminished. As a matter of fact it increased beyond her normal liking for the sweet just because chocolate was denied to her. When she went away to college, she was no longer under the watchful eye of her mother or her doctor; so she simply began a chocolate binge that never really ended despite a considerable weight gain and despite its deleterious effect on her acne. Her skin problem which never disappeared anyway became just a bit worse. Chocolate cookies (very chocolate and very sweet) for breakfast became a staple item in her diet for years and still is. You'll note that M. sought the very food she was prohibited from having while she was growing up.

Yet here is another absolutely true story that you may find even more amazing. After I had developed my diet plan I told a friend of mine a number of the "tips" outlined. When I mentioned the one about not giving up a favorite food he related this story about his son. "Jeff was a brighter than average boy but had a severe overweight problem. His favorite food was chocolate pudding which he cheated and had on any diet. The problem probably wasn't the chocolate pudding. What the problem was, once he cheated, he felt the diet wouldn't work and he continued to cheat with other foods. That's when I hit on the following idea. I told Jeff to go on a CHOCOLATE PUDDING DIET! To eat nothing but chocolate pudding; he loved the idea. At first he ate three dishes a meal. Even extra dishes while watching TV, and two before going to bed. After the third day I thought I'd made a mistake. It was my fear Jeff would blow up like a balloon. However, by day five just what I planned happened. He was sick of chocolate pudding. He begged to go on a normal diet. He went on that diet and stayed on it for some time. His big temptation in life was gone. What's even more interesting is that even now (years later) his desire for chocolate pudding is gone. In fact he gets sick when he looks at the stuff."

That story probably tells it best. Has there been a food in your life that is always the diet breaker? It might be a point to ponder.

PAUL MICHAEL WEIGHT-LOSS TIP #20 EAT 20% SLOWER AND YOU'LL SAVE 50% ON CALORIES. Have you ever noticed that thin people eat slowly? I was always the first one finished at dinner. There were even times when friends had hardly been served in a restaurant and I was done eating!

An obese man or woman rarely enjoys or savours the taste of food; he is usually too busy filling his stomach with more and more, turning the act of eating into not an act of pleasure but an act of compulsion, of habit, thus making him an unfree person. Teach yourself to become more discriminating in what you choose to eat; if a meal does not appeal to you, do not eat it. Don't abuse food. Taste it with pleasure and enjoyment and be sure you choose foods that are satisfying to your particular palate and craving. If you've been dieting well by eating high protein, low carbohydrate foods at various times of the day, or whenever you felt hungry, and then suddenly you have a terrific urge to devour a banana split, don't deny yourself this pleasure, for you will only feel depressed and anxious, and thus will possibly eat more of some other food. Of course you should be aware of the fact that you could eat only half the sundae or a third of it and still feel satisfied. Eat slowly and then test yourself when you have completed half the sundae and see if you have had enough, whether you feel quite satisfied, and if so, push the remainder away and get up from your seat. A healthier and slimmer you will be the result of your new self-awareness, of your new insight into your old eating habits.

PAUL MICHAEL WEIGHT-LOSS TIP #21 <u>FIND OUT WHEN YOU REALLY LIKE TO EAT AND EAT AT THAT TIME</u>. This little tip can save you a ton of carbohydrates. I'll have to give you another personal example. I love to eat during TV "cops and robbers" shows. I don't know what makes me that way I just know it's true. Maybe all the action gets me excited. Now, on Tuesdays and Sundays when I watch these shows, I have a light dinner and have my big meal during TV. In the past I simply ate my regular meal <u>AND</u> stocked in enough food for a TV crime show watching binge.

I'll give you another example of a friend of the family. Wilma, a thirty-six-year-old mother of three young children, knew that her overweight problem stemmed from her night eating. And it wasn't just snacking but real eating; she even bothered to heat up vegetables and other available leftovers. After the children were asleep, she ate these late meals in a room where she could be alone. Upon examining her attitudes toward eating and toward food (her reasons for overeating), she realized that her late night eating, in solitude, was the only time she truly tasted and enjoyed her food. At the dinner table, with the combined high noise level, the continual feeding demands from the children, and the serving and clearing away of dishes after each course led her to be unaware of what she was swallowing; she could have been eating anything. Wilma nibbled more than actually eating a complete meal at these times. Only later, in the quiet of a room could she take pleasure in eating. However, the result of this kind of routine was that she was eating two dinners, and one was late in the evening when her body could not transform that food into energy. After explaining to her family what her individual eating needs were, she merely drank coffee or wine during the family meal and consumed her own dinner in solitude later, thereby cutting down on her daily caloric intake and consequently losing weight permanently.

Knowing that you don't have to eat at an assigned time, that you can eat different foods from the rest of the family, and knowing that you can skip a meal when you are not hungry will give you the freedom to lose weight in a relaxed way and will enable you to avoid feelings of deprivation, hunger, and edginess, emotions commonly experienced when involved in most other diet programs. A young actress found that over the years she steadily gained weight, so that she was at the point in her career where only character roles requiring a fat woman were open to her. She felt that she had become overweight because she was eating too many meals a day, seven in fact.

The fault lay, however, not in her eating pattern (seven meals a day), nor did it lie in the fact that she felt free to eat, more or less, what she wanted. The trouble was that her diet was completely unbalanced, leaning heavily on the carbohydrate side. Often times she simply ate every three hours or so even if she did not feel real hunger. She had become a victim of poor eating habits and was unaware of them. In the morning she broke her fast by having only liquids (juice and coffee) which could only result in making her more hungry sooner, forcing her to con-sume too much at her next meal. Then as the day progressed, her meals got bigger and bigger and she completed her day about 11:00 p.m. with a sandwich and beer. Most of her daily portions of food included sandwiches, cakes and pies; very little protein, vitamins, and minerals that are so important in replenishing the body's nutrients. Yes, this "character" actress ate several meals a day but she picked food indiscriminately, and she consumed too much food (in the form of starches) at the end of the day, food which readily turns into fat. She never thought of skipping the appe-tizers at a party if she were not hungry. Freedom in eating in-volves insight into your nutritional needs and awareness of your eating habits.

PAUL MICHAEL WEIGHT-LOSS TIP #22 DON'T DIET ON VACATIONS.

Before you tell me that this is supposed to be a diet book let me explain. The diet outlined gives you plenty of chance for real eating that you will enjoy. Yet I know many of you will miss the cakes, the hero sandwiches and other starch/sweet foods. An occasional binge is not all bad. In fact goal setting is good. If you say to yourself "I'll stay away from sweets until my vacation in October" you are on the right track. This type plan will work for you for two reasons. First, because this type of planning gives you a goal to look forward to. Second of all, it's almost impossible anyway to diet on a vacation. So why break your diet and feel guilty about it? You'll notice a lot of this diet is designed to free you from the guilt you may have about eating. The plan lets you eat a lot (what you like to do) and it also lets you eat anything at times that it's impossible to diet.

PAUL MICHAEL WEIGHT-LOSS TIP #23 <u>WATCH THE SCALES</u>. One of the great advantages of the diet I propose is you'll see results in a hurry. You'll start losing weight in no time. Seeing that progress psychologically rewards you. Many heavy people have looked at the scale as their enemy. As a result they never use it or (in one case I know of) have thrown it away. Chart your progress daily. This doesn't mean to look for results at the end of the second day. But at the end of week two the results will give you the inspiration to stay away from that sweet you may want.

PAUL MICHAEL WEIGHT-LOSS TIP #24 <u>TAKE AN ALL PURPOSE MULTI-VITAMIN PILL</u>. One of the things you know is that you've given yourself every excuse for not dieting. One excuse that I used was that I "needed" all the foods I ate for my health. In reality the diet outlined in this report will give you more body building foods than you are now getting. But that isn't really the point. Taking vitamins will help you with your diet in that it will help you believe you are getting all the nutrients you need. In addition, if by some chance your meal planning does leave out some needed vitamins a multi-vitamin will supplement your diet. Incidentally, don't go wild buying expensive vitamins. So called natural vitamins are no better for you than regular vitamins. Just buy a bottle of one of those multi-vitamins and take one each day. You should buy the ones that contain minerals as well. By the way that little pill has almost no calories so don't worry about its effect on your diet. What follows is a listing of what effect vitamins have on your health. But remember too many vitamins are bad for you as well. So (unless your doctor says otherwise) just take one each day.

Here is a break down of the vitamins and their importance in your diet:

Vitamin A: Required for normal cell growth; it maintains resistance to infection, retards senility, increases longevity, benefits the eyes (lack of this vitamin could cause night blindness), the skin (without vitamin A, dry, rough skin results), the hair, organs and glands.

Vitamin B_1: Not enough of this vitamin will result in a lessening of hormones and a diminishing of sexual desire, dry hair, fatigue, sometimes irritability or constipation. It is also essential for normal digestive purposes and for growth of nerve tissues.

Vitamin B_2: Another name of this vitamin is riboflavin and its lack affects the eyes, the skin and proper functioning of the digestive track.

Vitamin B_6: Called pyridozine, it is needed to prevent a tendency to tooth decay, and is related to the metabolism of the essential unsaturated fat acids; its use will create good muscle tone, especially around the heart.

Vitamin B_{12}: This vitamin is the animal protein factor necessary for the growth factor in children and for the blood-forming function of bone marrow; it helps to prevent anemia and is important to the central nervous system.

Vitamin C (Ascorbic acid): Vitamin C is essential for bone formation and repair, tooth formation, proper healing of wounds, and it keeps the gums healthy as well as supportive and connective tissue.

Vitamin D: Lack of this vitamin results in the inability of the body to absorb calcium normally from foods, and poor teeth and poor bone structure will occur.

Vitamin E: Needed for the regular functioning of the cardiovascular system and is necessary for normal reproduction and the maintenance of sexual potency.

Vitamin K: Required for proper blood clotting and its lack can cause hemorrhages.

Along with the bodily requirements for vitamins are the minerals. The major minerals are calcium, iron, phosphorus, copper manganese, iodine, potassium and sodium. If there existed a deficiency of any of these minerals, the body function would suffer. The way the nerves send messages to your brain would be impaired, the water level, so essential to life processes, would be off balance.

PAUL MICHAEL WEIGHT-LOSS TIP #25 <u>DRINK LOTS OF TEA</u>. I found tea an excellent way to save me needless pounds. It wasn't until much later that I realized why it was such a great find. First of all unlike other diet foods it takes time to prepare. You've got to get out the old tea kettle, then boil the water and then let the tea steep. Once the process is complete you'll find tea a nice comfort. Tea tastes good to most people. With artificial sweeteners and lemon you can drink it by the vat full and it won't add an ounce. It also has the factor we talked about ... it keeps your mouth going and you swallowing. If you're like many folks you probably haven't had tea for years. You might think about rediscovering it. At about a penny a cup it's also one of America's best food buys. I still drink a dozen cups in a weekend. Best of all I'm drinking it instead of drinking cans of Cola.

PAUL MICHAEL WEIGHT-LOSS TIP #26 <u>CONCENTRATE ON WHAT YOU EAT; NOT HOW MUCH YOU EAT</u>. As well as your eating pattern I'm asking you to change your thinking pattern. In the past you were always concerned about the quantity of food you were eating. Now the quantity plays little importance. If you are deciding if you want to have the extra slab of roast beef or not ... go ahead and have it. By now I'm sure you've discovered one of the secrets of this diet. You no longer need willpower (the reason other diets fail). In addition, you will never feel a hunger pang or guilt about eating again. I always felt guilty after Thanksgiving ... not any more. You'll note from the carbohydrate counter that turkey has zero carbohydrates. This Thanksgiving I had plenty to eat. I simply ate lots of turkey and no stuffing.

This diet, you see, is really designed for people who love to eat. One of the interesting things about the diet plan frequently is that people have no idea you are dieting. This, of course, is a big help psychologically. Many diets (including this one) instruct you not to tell people you are on a diet. That's usually impossible when you are eating diet food. In the case of this diet it's very simple. Who would suspect you are on a diet when you sit down and devour eighteen spareribs or half a turkey.

A surprising fact, as you are cutting out carbohydrates you may (in the beginning) actually eat a little more food. Yet this food will not change to fat. In some of my early diet days I was eating meals like this:

Breakfast #1	Three eggs, three slices ham
Breakfast #2	A dozen sausage links
Lunch #1	Steak and huge salad
Lunch #2	Two medium lambchops
Dinner #1	Two 1½ lb. lobsters
Supper #1	Two hamburgers

Now here's the amazing part ... I was losing weight all the time!

Now I'm not suggesting you force feed yourself that quantity of food. I'm only pointing out that if you are a big eater you can still make it on this diet.

PAUL MICHAEL WEIGHT-LOSS TIP #27   <u>CUT OUT SWEETS FOR AN ENTIRE WEEK AND YOUR TASTE FOR THEM WILL DIMINISH.</u>   This is another fact that people usually challenge. The comment is frequently met with an outcry. I too thought I could not get by without cake. But the body has a number of interesting mechanisms working. Cravings are usually hardest to give up after the first day. Any alcoholic will tell you that once he makes it through the first day without a drink he's well on the way. The hardest part about giving up sweets is the first few days. On this diet you are allowed some carbohydrates. However, by starting with "cold turkey" treatment you make it easier for yourself later. Reading this now it may be hard for you to imagine but in a few short weeks you may prefer an extra slice of beef to an extra slice of pumpkin pie.

PAUL MICHAEL WEIGHT-LOSS TIP #28   <u>FOLLOW THE DIET CLOSEST IN THE FIRST TEN DAYS ... AFTER THAT IT WILL TAKE CARE OF ITSELF.</u> Closely related to the comment above is the fact that the first week is going to be the toughest for you. This is true not only in regard to sweets but in regard to all foods. Remember, I'm asking you to change a lifetime of habit. But like all habits, if you can make it through the first ten days ... you'll make it. It is going to take some extra concentration. If for the last eight years you've had a coffee and gooey pastry at 10 a.m. it is going to be difficult to change that pattern. However, ten days from now you'll be operating with an entirely new outlook ... and the weight loss to prove I was right.

What's coming up is the crossroads. The next ten days are the really difficult period. Make up your mind you'll get started and really follow through. All it takes is a little determination.

This special report gives you all the ammunition you need for weight loss. Now it's up to you to make it work. It's really quite simple once you get started.

PAUL MICHAEL WEIGHT-LOSS TIP #29 <u>DON'T LET MYTHS ABOUT WEIGHT LOSS KEEP YOU FAT</u>. Again we must deal with a psychological factor. You must remove from your mind any ideas about weight loss that may keep you from putting into plan the program outlined. Here are some common myths that need dispelling:

1.   It's healthy to be fat. (This is an old wives tale. The medical world has repeatedly informed you that being over-weight is a definite danger to your health; just think of all the strain extra fat puts on your vital organs.)

2.   I just have a natural tendency to be fat -- it's probably inherited. (Medically speaking, fatness as an inherited trait is rare; even if an individual is overweight because of a strong genetic tendency, he can still reduce through an effective diet and by changing his eating habits.)

3.   A glandular problem is the reason why I gain weight and I simply cannot lose pounds no matter what diet I follow. (Glands in themselves do not produce fat, and again, glandu-lar problems are rare. Actually, for the obese person, there is no glandular treatment; the only way you get fat is through overeating.)

4.   Whatever I eat turns to fat. (In reality only food that is not needed and not used by the body -- food in excess -- is stored as fat. Excess food high in sugar and starch content

is converted into fat and remains in widely distributed areas of your body.)

5. Even the intake of water makes me overweight. (Simply untrue. There is no way water can become fatty tissue.)

6. My stomach has stretched and requires a large intake of food. (The stomach is an elastic-type organ and will automatically change its size to accommodate the amount of food it receives.)

PAUL MICHAEL WEIGHT-LOSS TIP #30 WRITE DOWN ALL THE SUGARS AND STARCHES THAT YOU EAT FOR THE FIRST TWO WEEKS. That's right, I actually want you to carry a little pad and list all the starches and sugars you eat for the first fourteen days. Now remember, I haven't asked you to cut out all starch and sugar. I've just asked you to reduce them as much as possible. You may ask why I want you to write them all down. For two reasons. First, the act of writing down your carbohydrate intake will be a constant reminder to you of your eating pattern. Second, the system will point out how much sugar and starch you actually do eat. It really surprised me that I was consuming so much of the wrong type of food; it may surprise you as well. Don't write this off as just another psychological exercise. It's actually quite helpful in determining your diet pattern. This is especially helpful in the beginning stages of the diet.

PAUL MICHAEL WEIGHT-LOSS TIP #31 DON'T TRY AND SAVE MONEY ON FOOD. Let's face facts: high-protein diets are more expensive than high starch diets. Tuna costs more than toast. You are paying a price to lose weight. You're doing this for your health as well as any number of other family, social and personal reasons.

I want you to get over your fear of wasting money. If someone puts potatoes on your plate, it's okay for you not to eat them. Remember, you are going to eat again in a few hours. It's funny that the very people who will drop $10.00 on lunch at a fancy restaurant get concerned about throwing away thirty-five cents worth of french fries at home.

If you bought a paperback book for $1.50 and it turned out to be awful would you force yourself to read it because you'd spent $1.50? Of course not. If you bought a suit and it came with an ugly vest would you make yourself wear the vest with the suit because you paid for it? Of course not. Yet, you may have trouble not eating the free french fries that come with your burger. And what do you do with the free toast that comes with your two eggs?

You're going to have to learn to waste some food on this diet. This may be the hardest part of the diet. Yes, I too grew up with Mom telling me about those children starving in Europe.

Too many of us become human garbage cans. Sam Levenson jokingly says his mother "grew fat from shame." That is she ate what was left because it was a shame to throw it away. At home, hopefully, your mate will prepare only the right food. But watch out for "saving money" in restaurants.

PAUL MICHAEL WEIGHT-LOSS TIP #32 <u>A GOOD SEX LIFE IS PART OF A GOOD DIET</u>. This little-known tip can really help you. First, let me explain what I am <u>not</u> suggesting. If you are a happily married man I don't want you to rush out and find a girl friend. Rather I want you to understand that a good sex life can help you achieve your goal. In addition you should warn your mate that your sex appetite may increase as your food appetite decreases.

Let me explain. Fat people tend to be oral people. They like to talk, eat, chew. Psychologists tell us that oral people tend to be sensuous. Their senses are very important. We fat folk actually <u>enjoy</u> our food more than thin people. Sex therefore will be an asset to your diet. While some sense satisfactions may decrease we become more interested in others.

Without turning this report into a personal story, I'll relate one more that you may find familiar. In high school, if a girl didn't want to kiss me or rejected me in some other way I was off to the pizza parlor. Of course, this set off a vicious circle. The more I ate the more likely I was to be rejected and the more I was rejected the more I ate.

If you do have a sex partner now you are very lucky for this diet. If you do not, now might be an ideal time for you to become more social. Sensuous experiences tend to decrease your immediate need for food experiences. Get out of the house. The more social experiences you have the better off you'll be with this diet plan.

PAUL MICHAEL WEIGHT-LOSS TIP #33 <u>LOAD UP ON DIET HELP FOODS AND REDUCE ON SUGAR AND STARCH FOODS</u>. There is an interesting experiment a friend told me about. It seems scientists measured the number of times heavy people open their refrigerator doors versus the number of times thin people open the door. Can you guess the results? Sure enough, we heavy folk open the door to the refrigerator twice as often. That's twice as often to spot a nice piece of pie, a juicy apple, or leftover hero sandwich.

To succeed you should reduce temptation. If you live alone, tonight throw out all the starches, sugars and fruits in the house. Less to tempt you, the more chance to win.

If you live alone or with other people you also have to change your buying pattern. Load up the cabinets with canned fish; tuna, shrimp, salmon and the like. Keep the refrigerator filled with your favorite cheeses, corned beef, and other high protein foods. When you get hungry I want you to be able to choose from good diet foods.

The program is simple. Make it easy for yourself to win and difficult for yourself to lose. If two weeks from today I were to walk into your house I could guess the rate of your success by the contents of your shelves. It's not enough to avoid danger foods outside. Do everything possible to avoid them at home.

PAUL MICHAEL WEIGHT-LOSS TIP #34 <u>PLAN ON DOING A DAILY EVALUATION</u>. Don't get nervous. I'm not asking you to stay up all night evaluating your successes and failures. Rather take a minute or two to note the day's diet successes and failures. If you have had a number of successes, thinking about them will reinforce the possibilities of repeating them. If you have had any failures, noting them will help you from repeating them. For example, I actually saved extra carbohydrates (and therefore extra pounds) by changing the way I walked to work. I, in the past, walked by this city's most famous bakery. In my daily evaluation I learned this is where I fell apart. Changing my route was accomplished by practicing the daily evaluation routine.

A WORD ABOUT EXERCISE

Every diet book in the world cheers about exercise ... I don't. At the end of this report you'll note some simple exercises that take less than a minute a day!

First, let me say that no exercise program should be considered without consulting your family doctor. This is especially true for overweight people. Most doctors will tell you that overweight people have a tendency towards heart conditions and sometimes high blood pressure. For these people exercise can be dangerous.

Second, you're changing your entire eating pattern. To change your living pattern all at once may be too much for the psyche. Don't get me wrong. I believe in exercise, I even do it. I think it will be helpful for you to tone up your muscles and lose extra weight. But please note, THIS DIET PLAN DOES NOT REQUIRE EXERCISE TO WORK.

You'll help the plan along. Try the exercises at the end of the book. If you enjoy them I'm sure you'll find no shortage of exercises to perform. However, I do want to caution you about beginning a wild exercise program without your doctor's advice. I also want to caution you about "making yourself over" the first week after getting this report.

Now what about the value of exercise? Exercise has some physical and mental values. It tends to put your body "in shape."

It also has some tranquilizing value, it's a way of letting off steam.

At first exercise is going to be difficult. Start with the ones at the end of the report.

PLEASE, PLEASE DON'T GIVE ME ANY HELP

Lots of people think this is a fine diet. They start to lose weight on it and then for some unknown reason they decide to give the diet some help in working. This help comes in a number of forms.

Usually the form is special diet pills. There are hundreds on the market. They are available by prescription, by description, over-the-counter, under-the-counter and every which way. Let's get something straight. They will not help you, in fact they will hurt you on this diet.

This is true for a number of reasons. First, some diet pills in combination with a low-carbohydrate diet have a bad effect. The pill in combination with the extra fat you are taking in may actually cause the diet to backfire.

Second, is the long term problem. I'm going to take weight off you and keep it off. This diet will change your basic eating pattern and that's why it works. If your basic eating pattern is changed by the pills and not by you, the pattern will remain only as long as you take the pills.

Remember, I'm trying to smarten up your body chemistry. While these changes are going on we don't need any other chemicals mixing in there.

In case you haven't tried pills I can tell you that the medical experience is always that the weight loss is temporary. Also every week more and more doctors come out against them. The side effects are serious and long lasting. If it sounds like I'm trying to scare you out of taking diet pills ... you're right.

A WORD ABOUT WHAT'S DIFFERENT

"The sum is greater than the total of its parts" is a statement that has baffled math men for centuries. This diet works because it has hit on the right combination of elements which in total produce the desired effect. This diet will not work for you as well if you simply apply the principles separately.

Sure low carbohydrate diets work. There are numbers of them on the market. In addition, people have lost weight by applying psychologically sound principles to their eating. Even the idea of a lot of little meals instead of three big ones has shown good results. However, to get the maximum effect you must use this diet in combination. Follow ALL of the principles. They are laid out simply enough that it will not be difficult for you to follow them.

This diet is NOT just a revised low carbohydrate diet. Nor is it just one more thesis on why you eat a lot. It is a carefully worked out combination of those elements worked out for your success. Like all plans it must have all the elements working together. A chair is not a chair when it is some pieces of steel, some bolts and some fabric. The putting it all together is what makes it into a useful object.

Don't be deceived into believing that all of the elements are not important. Once you get the basic principles working together you'll succeed. To review; you'll eat a low carbohydrate diet; you'll eat six meals a day; and you'll apply the psychological principles in the second section of this report.

A FEW WORDS ABOUT RESTAURANTS

Restaurants are often the bitter enemy of the dieter. For me I really enjoy being on this diet. However, sometimes being put in a restaurant was a serious problem. Imagine telling a young child in a giant toy store that he could only choose from fifty per cent of the toys shown. In the psychological section of this report we deal with food and its meaning. One thing I already know about you; you really like food.

Restaurants are to the food lover as the European museum is to the art lover. Knowing this fact in advance can help us cope. Remember -- forewarned is forearmed. If restaurants are really your downfall then simply try to stay away from them. For some, because of business or family pressures, this is impossible.

To win in the restaurant game, here are a few tips:
A) Choose your battle grounds. A good general knows that he has an easier chance at victory if he's fighting on a safe terrain. This applies to the battle against grams of carbohydrates. A simple example is to stay out of a crepe restaurant. It's going to be very hard for you to find something interesting in a restaurant that features crepes. More thoughtfulness than ever before is

needed in your selection of a restaurant. For example, if a particular restaurant in your area is known for its lavish desserts stay away from it. My favorite "battle grounds" are seafood and steak restaurants. Remember, you're allowed almost any type of fish in unlimited quantity. My experience is that after you've put away a huge seafood cocktail followed by a filet in rich cheese sauce, a person just can't look at dessert. The same is frequently true for beef restaurants. Restaurants that call themselves steak houses usually feature large portions of beef. Frequently they offer a choice of a large or medium cut of meat. You know already which you should select. Filling up on beef is perfect for you. There are no carbohydrates at all.

B) Eat before you eat. This tip is my all important tip in the restaurant game. Remember the reason I suggested you eat six meals a day is so you are not overly hungry when you sit down at a meal. This is most important during eating out time. If you can walk into a restaurant and know you are not famished it will make ordering much easier. Also when it comes time to eat dessert you'll probably be truly filled. Simply put, if your first dinner is usually at 5 p.m. and the first supper at 9 p.m. you may want to slightly adjust the schedule on eating out nights. If dinner is planned at a restaurant for 9 p.m. simply change your first dinner to 7 p.m.

C) Watch out for ethnics. Every group has food that it is famous for. We Americans love to eat ethnic food. I've developed a love for Greek food while I have a neighbor who eats almost daily at a little Italian restaurant. Special planning is needed when eating ethnic food. It can either be your best friend or your worst enemy.

Here are some specific guidelines but let me establish one fact; you can find food to fit this diet in any restaurant, in any kitchen, anywhere in the world. The simple answer is to ask questions. There is nothing wrong with saying to a waiter, "Is that filet of sole prepared with flour?" or "Is the Captain's special cocktail prepared with sugar?" My experience is that waiters in ethnic restaurants are so used to the crazy diets and crazy illnesses of Americans that they will go out of their way to be helpful.

Italian restaurants are probably the hardest places to order on this diet. They are famous for their pastas. Even their meat dishes are frequently prepared in a flour base. And Italian pastries have enough sugar and flour to send a carbohydrates counter into near shock. But there is an answer. Italians are also famous for their delightful Antipasto. A large order contains less than one gram of carbohydrates. In addition they will be happy to prepare most any veal, chicken or beef dish on the menu without flour ... simply ask. Again, avoid temptation. But if you do find yourself in an Italian restaurant don't throw in the towel. You can still make it relatively carbohydrate free. And remember, when we decide we are losing we sometimes jump in with both feet. If you MUST have some baked ziti, okay, but there's no need to go wild and order every other hi-carb item on the menu.

Chinese food is our super-friend. If you like Chinese food

you are on your way to losing. They all feature a never ending array of shrimp, beef, lobster, duck, chicken and pork. It is important, however, to tell the waiter to leave out the cornstarch when preparing the sauces. The Chinese have a tendency to have a rather heavy hand with cornstarch. Leaving it out removes the heavy flavor and in the opinion of many gourmets its removal adds to the fresh light taste. Another bonus is that Chinese vegetables tend to be low in carbohydrates. As a matter of fact it's hard to make a mistake in a Chinese restaurant unless you are a rice eater.

French foods can present a problem. However, like our Italian ordering, simply specify cooked or sauteed in butter with no flour. The better French restaurants here (not true in Paris) tend to order good cuts of meat. You are therefore in good hands with almost any veal or beef selection.

The Jewish delicatessen features many meats, including brisket, pastrami, corned beef and tongue. All allowed in unlimited quantity.

In short, you can cope with restaurants ... simply plan and be prepared to order right.

OTHER CHANGES TO EXPECT

Our mental and physical health is affected by the foods we eat. With this diet you can look for some other signs that will tell you that you are on the right track.

For one thing by the end of the first week you'll find you have more energy. Part of what's been dragging you down are those starchy, heavy meals. Your psychological spirits will soar as your weight loss grows. It's interesting that people who eat this way simply tend to be more cheerful. At first, I thought I was just happy about the fact that I was losing weight. Later I noticed my spirits were generally improved.

A LITTLE ABOUT YOUR SYSTEM

Some individuals seem to lose weight the first day on this diet. Still others find that it's a week until they notice any appreciable weight loss. There are many factors that go into how quickly your weight loss will be. All I ask is a fair test. I'm sure at the end of week one you'll be losing weight. If you are a "tough loser" you can speed up the results. Try cutting down your carbohydrates a little more. If you are down to 60 grams a day, cutting it to 50 will give you some remarkable results. The important thing is not to become quickly discouraged. We all gain weight at different rates and we all lose weight at different rates.

SPECIAL TIPS ON GREMLINS TO WATCH OUT FOR:

1. Read labels carefully. Sometimes you are eating lots of carbohydrates and you don't even know it! This one fact can be a major problem on any diet, especially when foods that seem low in sugar are really jam packed with sugar. A good example is certain diet foods. For months I was drinking diet soda. One day I discovered it contained sugar. Sure, it had less sugar than regular soda but it still had too much. The one sure way to find out is to become a label reader. The government requires food

manufacturers to list ingredients. Don't assume anything, simply read ingredient statements.

2. Watch out for the combined effect of medications and this diet. Certain medications affect the working of this diet. For example diet pills are not an aid (but rather a problem) in combination with a low carbohydrate diet. If you are taking any pill on the advice of a doctor ask him what effect the pills will have on your diet and what effect the diet will have on your pills. If you are taking pills (like amphetamines or diuretics) on the assumption they will help you and not on the advice of our doctor, stop immediately. Most doctors will tell you that weight loss is difficult to achieve with pills and even in cases where you do lose weight the side effects aren't worth it. Anyway, you don't need pills to help you along with this plan, it works by itself.

3. If you're not hungry don't eat. Don't become so intrigued with the workings of eating six meals a day that you force yourself to eat. Keep in mind the tips about eating to be sociable and the like. One of the places that this diet falls apart is if the six meal idea becomes a challenge rather than a diet aid.

4. Learn what makes up carbohydrate foods. We are all accustomed to dieting in a certain way. This diet requires you to change your ways. Understand that certain foods (like fruits) are prohibited on this diet and can hurt the success. In other words re-read this report, and make sure you understand the program before you start.

ONCE YOU GET THERE

Once you achieve your desired weight ... my hearty congratulations. Now I want to make sure that you stay there. Chances
are you've broken many of the bad habits and eating patterns of
the past. Therefore staying at your desired weight won't be difficult.
One of the problems with old style diets is that even if they
worked, once you stopped the diet you were back to your old mis-
takes.

A lady wrote me and referred to my plan as the LIFETIME
DIET. Maybe this is the best name of all for it. The diet is really
a new approach to eating. You are satisfied and your body cells are
satisfied. For me, this diet is the way I eat all the time. I've
actually lost my taste for certain foods like ice cream and
certain rich desserts. They taste too sweet for me now. Sure, I
go on an occasional binge over a holiday period or while on vacation.
However, by and large, I return to this diet plan periodically.

It's easier to maintain your weight than ever before is
what I'm saying. The body fights for a condition of "maintenance."
If you take too much Vitamin C for example the body will expel
it. Our body as a system trys to "stay the same." This is the
reason you had so much trouble losing weight in the first place.
This is the reason I suggested no sweets for the first week; I
wanted to jolt your body into action.

Sometimes we find ourselves slipping back into old patterns.
That second morning breakfast again takes the shape of a gooey
pastry. Simply watch out for problems. However, now that you

know the secret of easy weight loss once you note the pounds coming back you can quickly switch into gear and start losing again with this program. Yes, it truly is a Lifetime Diet.

SET YOUR GOAL ... THEN PUT THIS DIET PLAN INTO ACTION. You have nothing to lose but unwanted pounds.

DESIRABLE WEIGHTS

Height		Small Frame	Medium Frame	Large Frame
		MEN		
Feet	Inches			
5	4	118-126	124-136	132-148
5	5	121-129	127-139	135-152
5	6	124-133	130-143	138-156
5	7	128-137	134-147	142-161
5	8	132-141	138-152	147-166
5	9	136-145	142-156	151-170
5	10	140-150	146-160	155-174
5	11	144-154	150-165	159-179
6	0	148-158	154-170	164-184
6	1	152-162	158-175	168-189
6	2	156-167	162-180	173-194
6	3	160-171	167-185	178-199
6	4	164-175	172-190	182-204
		WOMEN		
4	10	92-98	96-107	104-119
4	11	94-101	98-110	106-122
5	0	96-104	101-113	109-125
5	1	99-107	104-116	112-128
5	2	102-110	107-119	115-131
5	3	105-113	110-122	118-134
5	4	108-116	113-126	121-138
5	5	111-119	116-130	125-142
5	6	114-123	120-135	129-146
5	7	118-127	124-139	133-150
5	8	122-131	128-143	137-154
5	9	126-135	132-147	141-158
5	10	130-140	136-151	145-163
5	11	134-144	140-155	149-168
6	0	138-148	154-159	153-173

These weights apply to people over 25 years old. Figure light clothing and shoes when weighing yourself.

PSYCHOLOGICAL INSURANCE

Okay, everything is going along fine. You're losing weight and you're feeling good. Then boom, you wake up one morning and you don't feel like going on. Don't worry my friend, I've taken you this far and I'm not going to let you down. Here are a number of sure-fight and sure-fire ideas to keep you on the right track.

1) MAKE UP A "THIN BOOK" In this book paste pictures of models who are thin. People who look like you will look when you are thin. I use the men's catalog from Macy's to find pictures for my thin book. This serves as an inspiration. I also cut out clothes that I'll wear when I'm thin. One final note, then get up and look at yourself nude in a full length mirror. Now, ask yourself, which person are you? Keep your thin book around to refer to.

2) BUY AN EXPENSIVE GARMENT IN THE SIZE YOU WANT TO BE. I had a hand tooled leather belt in a size four inches too small. When the going got rough I asked myself, "Are you going to throw away the forty dollars you spent on this belt?" The answer was always an inspiration.

3) Get up and make labels with the carbohydrate counts for all the foods in the refrigerator. Stick the labels on the foods. I'm not sure why this works except that doing this little exercise focuses your mind on the problem at hand.

4) BUY YOURSELF AN EXPENSIVE PRESENT. Chances are the reason you may want to have a piece of pumpkin pie is that you think you need a treat. Well, give yourself a treat only make it a non-food treat. I bought my new camera just as I was about to pack in the diet ... and it worked. I stayed on the diet.

QUESTIONS AND ANSWERS

Here are some frequently asked questions and the answers to them.

Q. Does your diet mean I'll never be able to have chocolate cake again?

A. Never is a long time. This diet doesn't have to become a way of life. Sure after you lose the desired weight you can go back to your old style of eating. However, my best guess is you'll never want to eat like you did in the past. For you see you'll feel so much better as well as look so much better.

Q. What about yogurt? It's my favorite food.

A. Yogurt is fine ... as long as it's the unsweetened kind. You see once it's yogurt with blueberries chances are there is sugar added. Watch out for so called diet foods that are jam packed with sugar.

Q. What contains the most carbohydrates?

A. Sugar and flour. Lots of foods contain carbohydrate ... but avoid sugars and starches ... they are your worst enemies.

Q. Why do you say this diet will work while I've failed on so many others?

A. For a number of reasons (A) You'll be able to eat lots of food (B) You'll feel good instead of depressed (C) You'll see results right away.

Q. You mean calories have nothing to do with the diet?

A. I don't mean that at all. Calories do count but the most important thing is your carbohydrate count. Trying to keep calories down is important but don't become too interested in that. Just follow this diet and you'll lose weight.

Q. Should I see a doctor before I begin this diet?

A. Yes. Any change in diet requires medical advice. You will probably find your doctor is less than enthusiastic. However, as long as he agrees the diet is safe go ahead and get started. Most doctors we know tend to be conservative. Don't look for his blessing -- just make sure he agrees it's okay.

Q. I frequently have a bad taste in my mouth. Eating sweets helps me get rid of the taste. This is not true of eating proteins.

A. Many heavy people complain about a so-called bad taste. Interestingly enough most find it solved by mouthwash or strong toothpaste as well as by cake. If you are eating to solve a bad taste in your mouth, you're eating for the wrong reason.

Q. I've been told that overeating is in fact a mental illness. Shouldn't I see a psychiatrist?

A. Maybe you should. Maybe overeating is a mental illness. I'm not a doctor and I don't know. On the other hand, if this diet will solve your immediate problem (overweight) you may not need to deal with the cause.

Q. As a truck driver I really work hard, I need candy bars for quick energy.

A. Here's another myth sold to you by the sugar and candy companies. I have letters from people that tell me that when they approach a rough task they need that "quick energy." Sorry friend, it's all in your head. Scientific studies show it takes at least twenty minutes for your candy bar's energy factor to be absorbed into your bloodstream. Even pure sugar is not metabolized for fifteen minutes.

Q. My doctor tells me because of a variety of conditions I need a good deal of carbohydrates. Is he wrong?

A. No. This diet is designed for the average normal individual. If your doctor tells you that you have some special condition requiring special dietary considerations he knows you.

Q. I never seem to have enough at one sitting for dinner. I always crave more and usually it's sweets. Can you help?

A. One of the reasons this happens is that it takes time "for our stomach to tell our brain we are filled." In other words the brain hasn't gotten the message yet ... and we continue to shovel in food. There is a simple answer. I call it the mid-meal break. About halfway through the meal simply take a break. I actually have read a magazine and gone for a walk and then returned ... sometimes to find that I was no longer hungry. This (like many of these ideas) is a new eating idea; try it, it will work for you.

Q. What type of diet shall I tell people that I am on?

A. Don't tell them you are on a diet. Many well meaning friends may discourage you because this diet is unusual. If they find out tell them it's a "secret diet." That comment will let them know you are not interested in their help or ideas.

Q. Many of my friends are also on diets. They can't eat the rich cream sauces I'm allowed on my diet ... this causes problems.

A. I'm concerned with your problem not theirs. If they find your diet conflicts with theirs it's something they have to deal with not you.

Q. How much weight can I expect to lose on your diet?

A. Five pounds the first week, three to five the second week, and two pounds thereafter per week. Some people actually lose six pounds every week for the first two months. A lot depends on how much weight you are now carrying around. The report explains why you lose more first and less later. Be assured that YOU can reach your desired weight (whatever that is for you) on this diet. It may take you a little longer or a little less than average but don't be concerned.

Q. I notice I smoke less since being on this diet.

A. One of the basic effects of this diet is that people seem happier. As a result, they smoke less. Of course, smoking is a whole other problem. You are free to smoke as little or as much as you want without affecting the program.

Q. What do you think of Weight Watchers and other diet clubs?

A. I'm for any program that helps people lose weight. If clubs work for you, great. I support any healthy diet that trims away the pounds that make heavy people unhappy. However, it's been my experience that this diet will let you lose weight quicker and easier than any other.

Q. I'm pregnant. Can I use this diet?

A. No. Again, if you have any unusual condition consult your physician before beginning this plan.

Q. How is it possible that heavy cream is less fattening than milk?

A. Simple. Cream has more fat and less milk sugar by volume. Remember, we are trying to curb your sugar intake not your fat intake. This is another example of how you must retrain your thinking to be successful with this diet.

Q. My cousin tells me your diet won't work.

A. The world is filled with self-appointed experts on every subject. The world of dieting has more than its share. Some of the experts are well-meaning; others are quacks. I'm not interested in what anyone thinks except the readers of this report. The final judge of this plan must be the scale. YOU will know it works. I again warn you about confident experts in the field.

Q. The gram counter in your book is helpful but I'm interested in knowing the carbohydrate count of lots of other foods. How can I find out?

A. The best source of that information is a book by the United States Government. It lists literally thousands of foods and their carbohydrate count (as well as calories, fat, protein and vitamin value). The cost is only $1.55. To obtain a copy write: U.S. Government Printing Office, Washington, D.C. 20402. Ask for a copy of the "Department of Agriculture, Composition of Foods, Agriculture Handbook #8." As you can tell the government isn't big on snappy titles but the book is excellent.

Q. Don't people need fruits for good health?

A. What people need is the vitamin content of fruits, not the fruits. You get your required vitamins in the pill you take each day.

Q. Don't we need milk for good health?

A. Two-thirds of the world's people do not drink milk. You get all the nutrients that milk contains in the other foods you'll be eating.

Q. I find that on the weekends when I sleep late I don't have time to eat six meals. Is that okay?

A. Sure. Remember you only want to eat when you are hungry.

Q. I know you say no sugar, but how about natural or raw sugar?

A. I understand that raw sugar (unprocessed or less processed) is popular now in health food stores. However, you must recognize that raw sugar is still sugar with a few extra minerals. If you use it you must count it like regular sugar.

Q. I understand that sugar is needed for energy.

A. You understand wrong. For millions of years people ate no sugar and they had as much (probably more) energy as now. All of the fat we carry is nothing but stored energy.

Q. I'm a non-stop eater. I seem to be eating all the time. What can I do?

A. Without knowing you it's hard for someone to say why you

eat constantly. Look at the section on psychological tips. Even if all those fail, eating lots of protein will keep you slimmer than eating all those sugars and starches.

PAUL MICHAEL WEIGHT-LOSS TIP #35 <u>LEARN TO COUNT CARBO-HYDRATES THE WAY YOU PREVIOUSLY WERE TAUGHT TO COUNT CALORIES.</u>
You must learn to watch carbohydrates. That's the way this program will be a success. It may be a hard concept for you to break away from calorie counting and switch to carbohydrate counting. I've included a convenient list of foods and their carbohydrate count. There's no need to drag this list around with you. You'll note a few important facts. First, sugars and starches are carbohydrates. Fruits are very high in carbo-hydrates. Also watch out for grains of all types. Avoid cereals, corn, wheat and rice.

On the other side of the scale are foods that have low carbohydrates. You'll notice fresh meats contain no (or almost no) carbohydrates. The same is true of fats and oils. This will take some re-thinking as you were taught to stay away from fats and oils. Simply put, you should learn the basics of carbohydrate counting and carry a list to help check yourself in the beginning.

<u>CARBOHYDRATE GRAM COUNTER</u>

APPETIZERS

Caviar, 1 ounce	1.0
Clam dip, 3 tbsp.	1.5
Crab meat, ½ cup	1.9
Fruit cocktail (canned) 1 cup	39.4
Fruit cocktail (fresh)	12.0
Meatballs, 2 ounces	2.0
Mushrooms, ¼ lb.	5.0
Olives & celery 1 serving	2.0
Olives, green, 2 ounces	1.0
Olives, ripe, 2 ounces	1.0

CEREAL BAKED PRODUCTS

Animal cracker, 1	1.6
Cheese tidbits, 10	2.1
Cocoa graham, 1	5.7
Cookies (general), 1	20-40.0
Graham cracker, 1	5.4
Oyster crackers, 10	5.2
Ritz cracker, 1	2.0
Ritz cheese cracker, 1	2.0
Ry-Krisp, 2	9.6
Rye thins, 1	1.5
Saltine cracker, 1	2.3
Soda cracker, unsalted, 1	5.3
Wheat thins, 1	1.2
Zwieback, 1	5.4

DAIRY PRODUCTS

Butter, dairy, 1 pat (64 per pound)	tr*
Butter, dairy, 1 pat (45 per pound)	tr
Butter, dairy, 1 tbsp.	tr
Butter, dairy, ¼ cup	0.2
Butter oil, dehydrated, 7 tbsp.	0.0
Oleomargarine, 1 pat (45 per pound)	tr
Oleomargarine, ¼ cup	0.2
Margarine, ¼ cup hydrogenated	0.2
Cheese	
Blue mold, 1 oz.	0.6
Camembert, 1 oz.	tr
Cheddar, American 1 oz.	0.6

CEREALS

Bran flakes, 3/4 cup	22.6
Bran flakes, with raisins 2/3 cup	22.0
Cheerios, 1 cup	17.7
Corn flakes, 1 cup	21.0
Grape nuts, ¼ cup	24.0
Grape nut flakes, 3/4 cup	23.0
Rice Krispies, 1 cup	25.1
Special K, 1 cup	12.5
Wheaties, 1 cup	22.5
Wheat, shredded, 1 biscuit	18.3
Wheat Chex, ½ cup	23.4

COOKED CEREALS

Cream of Wheat, 1 cup	28.2
Farina, enriched, 1 cup	29.6

*A trace.

Oatmeal, 1 cup	26.0

CEREAL PRODUCTS

Egg noodles, 1 cup cooked	37.3
Macaroni, 1 cup cooked	42.2
Macaroni and cheese, 1 cup	45.3
Rice, brown, 1 cup cooked	38.2
Rice, white, 1 cup cooked	36.3
Rice, wild, ¼ cup cooked	21.1
Spaghetti, 1 cup	44.0
Spanish rice, 1 cup	24.9
Wheat germ, 1 oz.	13.1

BEVERAGES

Alcoholic

Beer, 8 oz.	10.6
Brandy, 1 brandy glass	0.0
Apricot brandy, 1 cordial gl.	6.0
Cider, 6 oz.	0.0
Cordial, anisette, 1 cordial glass	7.0
Creme de menthe, 1 cordial glass	6.0
Daiquiri, 1 cocktail glass	5.2
Eggnog, 4 oz.	18.0
Gin, dry, 1½ oz.	0.0
Gin ricky, 1 glass	1.3
Highball, 8 oz.	0.0
Manhattan, 3½ oz.	7.9
Martini, 3½ oz.	0.3
Old-fashioned, 4 oz.	3.5
Rum	0.0
Scotch	0.0
Tom Collins	9.0
Whisky, rye	0.0
Wines, dry, 4 oz.	1.0 - 5.0
Wines, sweet, 4 oz.	5.0 - 15.0

Common Beverages

Coca-Cola, 6 oz.	20.4
Ginger ale, 8 oz.	20.7
Pepsi-Cola, 8 oz.	27.6
Chocolate, all milk, 6 oz.	31.6
Chocolate milk shake, 8 oz.	58.0
Cider, sweet, 6 oz.	25.8
Coconut milk, 8 oz.	12.0
Coffee, clear, no sugar, 1 c.	0.8
Lemonade, 1 glass, 1 oz. lemon juice	27.2
Ovaltine, plain, 8 oz. milk	21.7
Postum, instant, clear 1 cup, 2 tbsp.	8.5
Soda, vanilla ice cream, regular	48.7

VEGETABLES

Asparagus, cooked 3/4 cup	3.6
Bamboo shoots, 3/4 cup	5.2
Beans, white, cooked 1/2 cup	21.2
Beans, lima, cooked 5/8 cup	19.8
Beans, green, cooked, 1 cup	6.8
Beets, cooked, 1 cup	6.0
Broccoli, cooked 2/3 cup	4.5
Brussel sprouts, cooked 2/3 c.	6.4
Cabbage, shredded, raw, 1 c.	5.4
Cabbage, cooked 3/5 cup	4.3
Chinese cabbage, shredded, raw, 2 1/4 cups	3.0
Carrots, 1 large	9.7
Carrots, cooked 3/4 cup	7.1
Cauliflower, cooked, 1/2 cup	4.1
Cucumber, raw, 1/2 medium	1.7
Eggplant, cooked 1/2 cup	4.1
Lettuce leaf, 3 1/2 oz.	3.5
Mushrooms, raw, 10 small	4.4
Mushrooms, sauteed, 4 med.	2.8
Mushrooms, canned 1/3 cup	2.3
Onions, raw, 1, 2 1/4" dia.	8.7
Onions, cooked, 1/2 cup	6.5
Onions, dehydrated flakes, 3 1/2 oz.	82.1
Onions, scallions, 5, 5 inches long	10.5
Parsley, 3 1/2 oz.	8.5
Peas, canned 2/3 cup	12.5
Peppers, green, raw, 1 large empty shell	4.8
Peppers, cooked, 3½ oz.	3.8
Pickle, cucumber, dill, 1 large	2.2
Pickles, bread & butter, 12 medium slices	17.9
Pickles, sour, 1 large	2.0
Pickles, sweet, 1	36.5
Potato, white, baked without skin, 2 1/2" dia.	21.1
Potato, boiled in skin, 1 medium	17.1
Potato, french-fried, 10	18.0
Potato, hash brown, 1/2 cup	29.1
Potato chips, 10	10.0
Rhubarb, cooked, with sugar 3/8 cup	36.0
Sauerkraut, 3/4 cup	4.0
Soybeans, cooked, 1/2 cup	10.1
Spinach, cooked, 1/2 cup	3.2
Sweet potato, baked, 1 large	58.5

Tomato, raw, 1 small   4.7
Watercress, 10 sprigs   0.3
Yams, ½ cup, cooked   24.1

MEATS

Beef (average serving)
    Brisket   0.0
    Filet mignon   0.0
    Flank   0.0
    Hamburger   0.0
    Heart   tr
    Kidney   2.0
    Liver, broiled   4.0
    Porterhouse steak   0.0
    Round steak   0.0
    Short ribs, braised   0.0
    Sirloin tip   0.0
    Stew   7.0
    T-bone steak   0.0
    Tenderloin steak   0.0
    Tongue   tr
Lamb (average serving)
    Chop, broiled   0.0
    Chops, loin, broiled   0.0
    Kidney   2.0
    Leg of, roasted   0.0
    Roast   0.0
    Shoulder roast   0.0
Pork (average serving)
    Chops, fried   0.0
    Chops, loin, center cut,
      broiled   0.0
    Ham, cured   0.0
    Ham, cured, shank end   0.0
    Leg roast   0.0
    Liver   4.0
    Loin   0.0
Chicken (average serving)
    Barbecued   tr
    Braised with dressing   29.0
    Baked   0.0
    Boiled   0.0
    Gumbo   0.0
    Paprikash   0.0
    Roasted   0.0
Duck (average serving)   0.0
Turkey (average serving)
    Dark meat   0.0
    White meat   0.0
    Gizzard   0.0
    Hash   8.0
    Roasted   0.0

MEAT, PROCESSED

Bacon, crisp, 1 strip	0.2
Bacon, Canadian, raw, 1 slice	0.1
Beef pot pie, 4¼ in. dia.	37.0
Bologna, 1 slice	1.1
Chicken pot pie, 3 3/4 in. dia.	40.3
Chili, no beans, 5 oz.	6.7
Corned beef hash, ½ cup	9.3
Deviled meat, 1 tbsp.	tr
Frankfurter, 1	1.0
Liverwurst, 1 slice	0.5
Luncheon meat, 1 slice	0.5
Polish sausage, 1 slice	0.0
Scrapple, 3½ x 2¼ x ¼ inches	26.0
Sausage, beef and pork, 1	0.0
Vienna sausage, 1 average link	0.0

NUTS

Almonds, unblanched 12 to 15	2.9
Brazil, shelled, 4 med.	1.7
Cashews, roasted, 6 to 8	4.1
Coconut, shredded, 1 cup	13.6
Garbanzos, ½ cup	61.0
Macadamia, roasted, 6	1.5
Peanut butter, 1 tbsp.	3.0
Peanuts, raw, 3½ oz.	21.3
Soybeans, ½ cup	33.5

SALAD DRESSING

Blue cheese, 1 tbsp.	1.0
French, 1 tbsp.	2.4
Italian, 1 tbsp.	1.0
Mayonnaise, 1 tbsp.	0.3
Thousand Island, 1 tbsp.	2.2

FAT AND OILS

Bacon fat, 1 tbsp.	0.0
Chicken fat, 1 tbsp.	0.0
Corn oil, 1 tbsp.	0.0
Cottonseed oil, 1 tbsp.	0.0
Lard, 1 tbsp.	0.0
Olive oil, 1 tbsp.	0.0
Peanut oil, 1 tbsp.	0.0
Safflower oil, 1 tbsp.	0.0
Soybean oil, 1 tbsp.	0.0
Suet, beef, 1 tbsp.	0.0

FISH AND SHELLFISH

Abalone, canned, 3 1/2 oz.	2.3
All fish, raw, broiled, sauteed	0.0
Caviar, 1 round tsp.	0.5
Lobster, whole, 3 1/2 oz.	0.5
Lox, 1 oz.	0.0
Oysters, raw, 5 to 8	3.4
Sardines, canned in oil, 8 med.	0.6
Shrimp, raw, 3 1/2 oz.	1.5
Tuna, canned in oil, 3/4 cup	0.0
Tuna, canned in water, 3/4 cup	0.0
Turtle, green, raw, 3 1/2 oz.	0.0

FRUIT

Apple, 3-inch dia.	33.4
Applesauce, 1/3 cup	23.8
Apricots, raw, 2 to 3	12.8
Apricots, canned, 3 halves	22.0
Avocado, half, 3¼ x 4 in.	6.3
Banana, 1 large	44.4

DESSERTS

Cake

Cake, angel, 1 piece	27.1
Fruitcake, dark, 1 slice	23.9
Pound cake, 1 slice	14.1
Sponge cake, no icing, 1 piece	27.0
White cake, no icing, 1 piece	27.0

Pie

Apple, 1/6 of 9-in. pie	61.0
Banana custard, 1/6 9-in. pie	49.2
Boston cream pie, 1 serving	54.9
Cherry, 1/6 of 9-in. pie	61.5
Coconut custard, 1/6 of 9-in.	38.5
Custard, 1/6 9-in. pie	35.1
Lemon meringue, 1/6 of med.	52.8
Mince, 1/6 med.	66.0
Peach, 1/6 med.	63.0
Pecan, 1/6 med.	82.0
Pumpkin, 1/6 med.	36.7
Raisin, 1/6 med.	32.5
Rhubarb, 1/6 med.	61.2

SUGARS AND SWEETS

Brown, dark, 1 cup	210.0
Brown, crude, 1 tbsp.	12.7
Corn, unrefined, 3½ oz.	90.0
Maple, 1 piece	13.5

powdered, 1 tbsp.	10.9
White, granular, 1 tsp.	4.0
White, granular, 1 tbsp.	11.9
White, granulated, 1 cup	199.0
Apple butter, 1 tbsp.	9.1
Assorted jams, comm., 1 tbsp.	14.2
Assorted jellies, comm. 1 tbsp.	11.3

LIQUID DIET FOODS

Metrecal, 8 oz.	27.5

BREADS

Biscuit, 1, 2-inch dia.	16.0
Bran-raisin, 1 slice	27.2
Corn bread, 3½ oz.	32.9
Cracked wheat, 1 slice	12.0
French toast, 1 slice	14.1
Hamburger bun, 1	15.9
Pumpernickel, 1 slice	17.0
Rye, 1 slice	12.0
Tortilla, 1, 6-inch dia.	13.5
Waffle, plain, 1	28.1
White enriched, 1 slice	11.5
Whole wheat, 1 slice	11.0

PAUL MICHAEL WEIGHT-LOSS TIP #36 KNOW THE POISON FOODS

AND AVOID THEM LIKE THE PLAGUE. There are certain foods that are really bad for you implementing this diet plan. Know these foods and avoid them. If need be make a copy and keep this list in your wallet.

Bananas	Honey
Bread	Ice Cream
Cake & Cookies	Milk
Candy	Pancakes
Cereal	Pasta
Corn	Rice
Dates & Figs	Sugar

PAUL MICHAEL WEIGHT-LOSS TIP #37   <u>KNOW THE OKAY FOODS SO</u>

<u>IF YOU GET HUNGRY YOU CAN EAT AN EXTRA PORTION.</u>   These foods are

okay.   In fact you can consume them in any quantity.

Steak	Chicken	Any fish
Chops	Turkey	Eggs
Beef	Duck	Cheese (except soft cheese like cream cheese)
Hamburger	(in fact, any fowl)	Butter & Margarine
(in fact, any meat except cold cuts)		Mayonnaise or Salad Dressing (no sugar)

PART 2: PHYSICAL EXERCISE WITHOUT MOVEMENT

A new method of exercising has been developed which is particularly suited for supplementing daily activity. Now you can strengthen your muscles to a degree previously achieved only through a much lengthier program of very strenuous activity.

Using the nine basic exercises described here, you can work toward physical fitness sitting down -- and in just 54 seconds a day.

The secret of this method is in using one set of muscles to exercise against another. By this method you can strengthen and tone your muscles without any actual body movement at all.

And you only have to devote six seconds to each set of muscles. Why only six seconds? Because in only six seconds most people can gain a significant amount of strength and muscular tone.

Science has shown us that a muscle can grow in strength only at a certain rate. This rate can't be speeded up, no matter how much you exercise beyond a certain point.

NINE WAYS TO TAKE YOUR EXERCISE SITTING DOWN

Just a minute, please! That's the length of time it takes to perform all nine of these exercises.

Hold your breath while you do each exercise -- and do each one for six seconds. Then relax completely for a few seconds before going on to the next exercise.

IMPORTANT: For the first week apply only about 50% maximum effort in these push or pull positions -- maintaining tension for approximately six seconds only in each position.

For maximum benefit these exercises must be performed every day. Although a single repetition in each position will result in a significant increase in strength for most individuals, several repetitions will improve your muscular endurance and provide an even greater strength increase.

By rigidly adhering to this method of exercise, some people have doubled their strength in only 20 weeks. The average increase is between 3% and 5% per week.

The nine exercises below have been designed specifically for people who do not normally get a great deal of exercise. The only equipment needed is a chair and a table -- plus initiative, pride and desire!

YOUR 9 EXERCISE PROGRAM FOR BETTER HEALTH

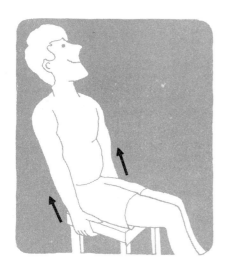

EXERCISE #1

THE PULL-UP -- for your arms and shoulders. Sit straight and grasp the sides of your chair tightly with both hands and pull up as hard as possible.

EXERCISE #2

THE HAND PRESS -- for your arms, chest and shoulders. Sit straight with chest out and arms held across your chest. Place one fist inside the other. Press together using all the strength of your arms and your shoulders.

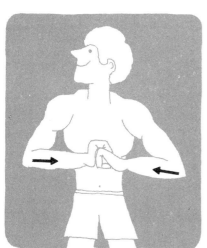

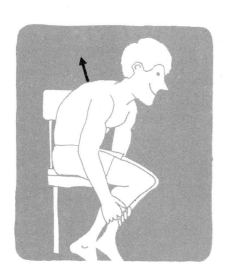

EXERCISE #3

THE BACK PULL -- for your lower and upper back. Keep your back straight and lean forward until you can grasp your legs or braces of the chair. Pull straight up using your back muscles only.

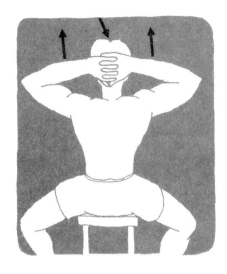

EXERCISE #4

THE NECK PRESSER -- for your neck.
Sitting straight, clasp your hands
behind your neck holding elbows
forward. Pull forward with your
hands and at the same time press
your head backward.

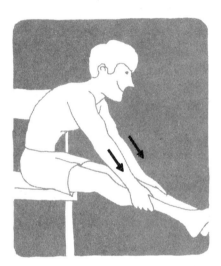

EXERCISE #5

TUMMY TIGHTENER -- for your waist
and abdomen. Sitting with legs
together straight out, bend forward and grasp your legs just
below your knees. Press down with
your hands, at the same time press
up against your hands with both
legs.

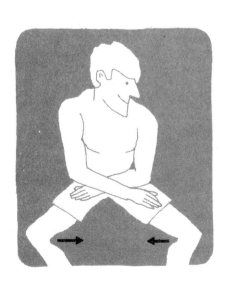

EXERCISE #6

THE CRISS-CROSS -- for your chest
and legs. Placing your feet about
4 inches apart, bend forward and
place your hands against the inside of opposite knees. Attempt
to press your knees together while
at the same time holding them apart
with your hands.

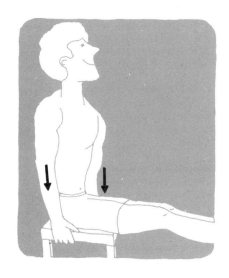

EXERCISE #7

<u>THE BODY LIFT</u> -- for your shoulders, arms and abdomen. Keeping your back straight, lean forward and place your hands against the sides of the chair. Hold your legs straight out and try to raise your body about 1 inch off the chair.

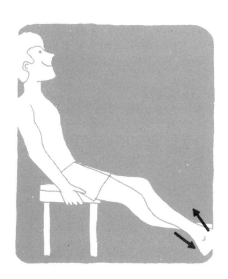

EXERCISE # 8

<u>THE LEG SQUEEZER</u>. While sitting forward on the edge of your chair, lean back, hold legs straight out. Hook one foot over the other and hold tightly. Rest your feet on the floor, keep legs straight, then try to pull feet apart.

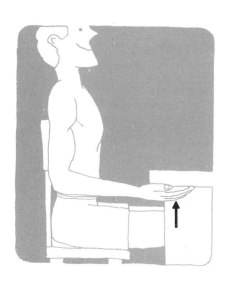

EXERCISE #9

<u>THE ARM CURL</u> -- for your upper arms. Sit straight, grasp the underside of a heavy table or desk with your palms up, forearms parallel to the desk or table. Push up as hard as possible.

A FINAL WORD

You are now about to embark on your last diet. Throw away your pills, your diet books, and your diet foods. Reread this report once and then get started. Any one of the tips in this report saves you ten-twenty-thirty pounds. The diet works.

One final review before you get started. Here are the five most important aspects of the diet.

1. Keep your carbohydrate count below 60 grams a day.

2. Eat lots, yes lots, of high protein foods.

3. Eat six meals a day.

4. Take a multi-vitamin every day unless your doctor has told you otherwise.

5. Take the psychological suggestions in this report to heart.

GOOD LUCK ... I look forward to hearing from the happier, healthier, thinner, new you!